"They don't pay off on eff[...]
And BE A BEAST will get y[...]

— **Harvey Mackay**, #1 New York Times bestselling
author of *Swim With The Sharks Without Being Eaten
Alive*

*"Read BE A BEAST and learn why success in life is
really an inside job."*

— **Ken Blanchard**, co-author of *The New One Minute
Manager®* and *Refire! Don't Retire*

*"I've spent a lifetime pursuing excellence in both my
personal and professional life and BE A BEAST is not
just another tool to help me attain my goals...it is the
tool that I use myself and recommend it to anyone
seeking to improve their performance in every aspect
of their life."*

— **COL Michail S. Huerter**, US Army Ranger
Garrison Commander

*"The keys to winning in every aspect in your life are
contained within the pages of this book."*

— **Warren Moon**, NFL Hall of Fame quarterback and
founder of Sports 1 Marketing

*"Your animal instincts are powerful, intrinsic, and
useful given Roger and Dave's brilliant tools that will
help you to drive yourself to ever greater successes."*

— **Mark Victor Hansen**, co-author of the bestselling
Chicken Soup for the Soul series

*"Both Dave and Roger are two of those rare
individuals who not only can 'talk the talk' but also
'walk the walk.' They have a tremendous base of
knowledge that is laid out beautifully in this book."*

— **Bill Bartmann**, NY Times #1 bestselling author and
self-made billionaire entrepreneur *Bail Riches*

1

"Dave Austin, along with his partner Roger Anthony, have once again 'hit it out of the park.'"

– **Dennis Kuhl**, chairman Angels Baseball

"When you change your mindset...you change your life. In BE A BEAST, Dave Austin and Roger Anthony share a fresh, entertaining and actionable perspective on how you can quickly identify what is holding you back, and provide tools that will help you stop outside circumstances from controlling your life...allowing you to seize control of your future. This process will allow you to ignite your inner genius and create great success and joy in your life."

– **Sharon Lechter**, bestselling author of *Think and Grow Rich for Women*, co-author of *Outwitting the Devil, Three Feet From Gold* and *Rich Dad Poor Dad*.

"Dave works like no one I've ever seen before. But then again, he's the most effective of anyone I've ever seen in this field."

– **Jim Tracy**, MLB 'Manager of the Year' 2009,
Colorado Rookies

"All elite performance driven individuals, whatever their arena is, will benefit from implementing this unique, unconventional, and edgy approach to higher achievement. Its decisive framework and method for maximizing performance is 'one of a kind' and simple to learn and integrate immediately. As an Army officer competing in the 60-hour non-stop 'Best Ranger Competition,' Dave's coaching and mentorship gave us the edge we needed to cross the finish line."

– **Trevor Shirk**, Captain US Army Ranger

"In order to become a champion, you must think like a champion. The principles of RESPA were tools I used while competing for the gold medal at three different Olympics. In this book, Dave and Roger hit a home run when it comes to teaching you how to become a beast in all areas of life."

– **Leah O'Brien Amico**, 3-time Olympic Gold Medalist and 3-time National Champion, USA softball

2

"I really love how BE A BEAST gives you a deeper connection to goodness."

– David Meltzer, CEO Sports1 Marketing, author of *Connected to Goodness*

"Every athlete needs the right frame of mind to bring out the best in themselves. Both Dave and Roger have brought amazing experience and knowledge to this BE A BEAST book to help you unleash your inner beast through the extreme focus and mental strength that is necessary in order to give yourself the best chance to compete at your highest level."

– Jeff Garcia, 17-Year NFL All-Pro quarterback

"BE A BEAST – how can it get better than this?"

– Greg S. Reid, bestselling author and filmmaker

"As an organization that keeps the military community and our mission first living our core values, it is often difficult to find a book that can take an already high performing group to the next level...but that is what we have found with BE A BEAST. Your system for developing focus, composure and the highest quality output based on a shared core belief system has catapulted my group to be one of the highest performing teams at USAA. Even more importantly, we have come to trust, care and rely on each other as only a family would. As a leader at USAA, it's one of my key responsibilities to create conditions for people to succeed....you have enabled me to do that...for which I am sincerely grateful. Your program teaches life skills that we will carry with us in whatever endeavors we pursue.

– Kristin Shelt, director of market research and competitive intelligence for USAA

"Dave and Roger have opened my eyes to a whole new level of coaching. Thanks so much for these pages of such tremendous reading filled with great wisdom."

– Ted Cottrell, 25-year NFL coach

"BE A BEAST is not only game changing, it is life changing. These principles helped me lead our team from having the worst record (4-14) in 2013 to having the best record in Arena Football history (17-1) in 2014, which was followed by our franchise's first Arena Bowl Championship appearance."

– **Shane Austin**, AFL quarterback and certified 'Extreme Focus' coach

"Dave Austin has a distinct genius in guiding professionals to greatness, athletes and business people alike. BE A BEAST is a 'must read' which provides a powerful framework that will empower you to access your potential to achieve any and all of your dreams."

– **Mary Manin Morrissey**, bestselling author of *Building Your Field Of Dreams* and the founder and CEO of Life Mastery Institute

"As a sports agent and being involved in athletics my whole life, I have come to learn how important having the right mental mindset is in playing at the highest level. BE A BEAST gives you great tools to stay focused under pressure and is filled with unique mind-triggers to keep you dialed in."

– **Bruce A. Tollner**, co-author of *Sidelined: Overcoming Odds through Unity, Passion and Perseverance* with Chuck Pagano and Tony Dungy, and co-founder of REP 1 Sports agency

"BE A BEAST is the epitome of a crash course MBA in extreme mental focus. These are the keys to harnessing the unlimited power of your mind, body and spirit! The sound principles and wisdom which Dave and Roger share in the pages of this text, will become the bible of every 'team' reaching for success, whether it be in the boardroom, on the field, or on the stage of life. We are all athletes of life, so get your Beast Mode ON!"

– **Jeff S. Brodie**, founder and managing partner of Zero Problem Computing and Codefusion Communications, Inc.

"These BE A BEAST principles aren't just for professional athletes, they are for the executive in the boardroom who needs to make a critical decision. They are for the call center agent who needs to reset their mind and heart to serve the next customer. They are for the front desk agent or retail clerk who are literally the face of their company. Everyone in every company is on the field every day, all day. There are no second chances. Today, business is as fast as the 92 MPH fastball thrown by a professional pitcher. Everyone on your team from the boardroom to the showroom needs to be peak performers. They need the mental focus and emotional resilience tools that the BE A BEAST book provides."

– Tony Bodoh, customer service specialist to Fortune 100 and 500 companies

"I met Dave roughly 10 years ago. It was during the recruiting process of his son to the University of Hawaii, and right away I felt he had a different energy. We talked about some of the key things in the BE A BEAST book back then. Dave got IT. And that IT that most have a hard time putting a finger on, is captured in the pages of this BE A BEAST book.

As we got to know each other, we realized that so many of the things we do on the football field with my team, directly transfer to a successful business and a successful personal life.

Things that I have used for 30 years in coaching football both in the NFL and at the college level were great to read in his book. His 12-step process is a formula to reach the highest level of performance.

Aristotle said this about success, 'We must manage our behavior to meet the objective. We are what we repeatedly do, excellence then is not an act but a habit.' You must do whatever that is over and over to execute without actually having to think about it.

In order for an athlete or any person trying to play the game at the highest level, one must be able to execute under the most extreme conditions without having to think about it. There is no time to think when you are being rushed as a quarterback on 4th and 1.

It is what my teams call executing with 'unconscious competence.' And the only way you can play the game at the highest level is to repeatedly do over and over whatever is the technique required for your position, and then do it faster and quicker than your opponent does his technique. It just happens naturally. You do not have to think about it. You have done it so many times before, it just happens naturally.

As Colin Powell, first African-American commander of our troops says, 'There are only two things you have to have to be the best, one is opportunity and two is proper training.' The BE A BEAST book gives you a plan to do this. It's what every successful athletic team does, and as I said will transfer to both business success and personal success as well. Everyone simply must read BE A BEAST."

– **June Jones**, former NFL quarterback and head coach of both the *Atlanta Falcons* and *SD Chargers*

"If you are looking for the next best thing in your life to change everything that relates to getting results you want out of your life, BE A BEAST is where you start. It will bring you to your 'A' game."

– **Berny Dorhmann**, Chairman CEO Space, Inc.

"You could never pay enough for the value our team has received from this style of 'mental conditioning' coaching. This work is priceless."

– **Shiv Jagdav**, head coach for USA's Olympic field hockey team during the World Cup Competition

"In law enforcement it is crucial to stay alert and focused, while maintaining complete control in pressure situations. As with all first responders, we are tasked with making split second decisions that could mean the difference between life and death. BE A BEAST is a great resource that provides important mental tools for our trade."

– **James Slayter**, law enforcement professional,
Honolulu, Hawaii

6

"BE A BEAST – the perfect and most natural way to fully connect and engage to our natural instincts and deepest desires, to then act boldly towards achieving our overall vision and goals."

– **Efrat Avnor**, mental performance and certified 'Extreme Focus' coach, Israel

"Here's how I know that the BE A BEAST principles work; I took notes and kept a notebook of all my meetings with Dave. I wrote down the key content of our meetings and now I carry it around with me all the time. I constantly pull up the resources from the BE A BEAST book to prep me before my biggest challenges! That way I'm always 'game ready!"

– **Christopher Veum**, president AVRP Studios

"Young Brothers worked extensively with Dave Austin during the time of the last big recession and when the shipping company was going through a number of organizational changes, which included several new faces that were relatively new to the industry. We had a great opportunity to knit our team together into an interdependent unit, to understand each other, and to know how we could count on helping one another. Fortunately, Dave was able to spend time in Hawaii and consult with us individually and collectively. Our corporate retreat was extraordinary resulting in a new meaning for the Young Bros! Many of the concepts he taught us are in BE A BEAST. There is something in this book for everyone, and hopefully a lot of it."

– **Glenn Y. Hong**, president Hawaiian Tug & Barge Corp. and Young Brothers Limited

"I really love the BE A BEAST principles presented within this book. Dave worked with our team as we pushed the limit and built out the largest longest running conference in America...and personally used these animal triggers with great results. I am excited now that everyone gets to learn more about these extremely powerful mental mindset tools."

– **Michelle Patterson**, CEO of Women Network and president of the California Women's Conference

"This process takes you to championship level before you even walk out on the field. You will win before you play. BE A BEAST is your playbook to success."

— **Garrett Gunderson**, #1 NY Times Bestselling author and financial strategist *Killing Sacred Cows*

"I've worked with Dave as a Major League Baseball player and now as a businessman, and the greatest lesson that I've learned from the principles that are found in the BE A BEAST book...is that life is about less words and more heart."

— **Jason Botts**, former MLB player and founder of the FULL FORCE Life

"I'm a firm believer in these philosophies and tools as I already try to live by the power of positive thinking as much as possible. Your program helped me to put things into perspective in terms of sports marketing."

— **Pam Frasco**, VP marketing and communications for the Cleveland Cavaliers and Lake Erie Monsters

"One of the reoccurring things I kept thinking about is the importance of positive thinking and "Champions are Champions before they were Champions." I have always known having the right mindset is one of the most important things you can have, but often haven't given that concept as much credit as it deserves. I've put equal (maybe even MORE) value into putting in the work and repetition in getting better at whatever you are trying to accomplish. In the BE A BEAST training I learned to never discredit the power of positive thinking and using daily affirmations."

— **Alan Mowrey**, VP franchise development for the Cleveland Cavaliers

"It was during a rough stretch in my business that I began working with Dave as my personal mindset coach. I now believe so strongly in these principles that I can't wait to give my entire staff and family his new BE A BEAST book."

— **Thomas Justus**, CEO, ICS, Inc.

"Dave does a great job of articulating the key principals of success that can be applied to any passion, profession or sport. The concept of learning how to BE A BEAST is easy to understand, and more importantly, easy to retain and put in to action. These foundational concepts are shared by many of the most successful people in the world, and through this book Dave provides everyone with the keys to unleash your inner beast!"

– **Kelly Foy**, founder and former CEO of Elite
Meetings International

"The 'Best Ranger' competition is the elite of the elite of the Army. It is the toughest competition out there in the world. It is three days 70 miles, limited food, limited sleep. Limited sleep means about 1 and 1/2 hours sleep over the 36 hours. It was physically and mentally the toughest thing I have ever done in my life. I don't think without the BE A BEAST training I would have gotten through. We sang out our intentions during the rock marches, it got us fired up. At our lowest low those mantras helped pull us out of the darkness. Thank you for giving us the mental tools to bring us through."

– **Kevin Raymond**, Captain US Army Ranger

"BE A BEAST provides an expansive and much-welcomed exploration of what drives us and how we can harness that knowledge for greater passion and success. Dave and Roger have created an invaluable resource. The authors developed a keen appreciation for human potential early in life, and have put into words lessons for us all: through awareness of our own nature we can set our intentions and live with greater purpose and joy. By applying the lessons of this book, living with integrity, success, and passion will become habitual. Essential for anyone looking to improve in business and in life!"

– **Marshall Goldsmith**, author of the *New York Times and Wallstreet Journal* #1 Best Seller *Triggers*

BE A BEAST

Unleash Into Your Animal Instincts

For Performance Driven Results

Book One

Dave Austin and Roger Anthony

with Cathy Lynn

Dedication

"To our brother Roger Anthony, his legacy, and a lifetime body of incredible and inspirational work."

– Dave Austin and Cathy Lynn

Although we had known each other for what seemed like lifetimes, Roger and I had the pleasure of working together, on and off, for about 7 years. And, during the last two years we were graced with Roger's physical presence, I am blessed to have called him a business partner—but more importantly, a dear friend and great mentor. There are very few people I would put in a class of mastery, and Roger was one for sure. He taught me an enormous amount about life—and things that mattered, such as courage, humility, and integrity.

Many who personally knew Roger, also knew that he had earned the nickname of "Mr. Integrity," and for good reason. I have never met anyone who had more integrity than he—it actually oozed out of his body. My heart, as well as those of many, many others, bled deeply during the spring of 2014—that was when one of our greatest teachers, mentors, and guides was called back home. We treasure your legacy of learning through animals and from the beauty nature itself, and gracefully walk in the footsteps you've left behind.

Brother Roger, this book is dedicated to you and your lovely wife, Cindy. May you continue to "be a beast" in all that you do, and wherever you go. We feel your presence in this work as if you were still standing here by our side—and we are so very grateful to have you a part of both the BE A BEAST extended family and our personal family as well. You are forever in our hearts and will cherish your mentorship and friendship for all-time and forever.

"In life and in sports, having the right mindset is essential. Be A Beast supplies the tools to win in every aspect of life."

Table of Contents

"Be A Beast goes way beyond sports; this applies to life and living a life of excellence."

Foreword

For me, any book that teaches you the results you get are in direct relationship to your daily habits is a great read. That's just one of the many reasons I think you should read *Be A Beast*.

I've been talking about the effects that paradigms (a multitude of habits) have on results for more than 45 years. Dave and Roger do a marvelous job of illustrating the connection between the two in this book.

I also love that *Be A Beast* teaches you how to stop letting the outside world control your life, which is what the vast majority of people do.

You see, from a very young age we are taught to live by what we see, hear, smell, taste, and touch in our outside world. So we're constantly bombarded by external stimuli and countless circumstances that are beyond our control. Instead of letting our senses and the outer world control us, we need to tap into our higher faculties, our inner world.

The third thing that stands out about this book is its ability to help you get a clear vision of what you want and start living into your dreams, rather than ignoring or running away from them.

Far too often people talk themselves out of their dreams. They don't see how they're going to achieve them so they keep backing away until they have an easier goal that they already know they can achieve.

This book helps you see how you can—and should—go after something you really want.

Be A Beast helps you "light the fire from the inside out" by giving you a proven 12-step process to use. You'll learn practical steps that can be incorporated into your daily life and, through practice and repetition, create new thought patterns and productive habits.

This process helps you move from where you currently are to where you ultimately want to be. This book is an excellent investment. Everything it advocates is backed by years of research and real-world experience on athletic fields and in corporate boardrooms.

The principles presented on these pages will work whether you're an entrepreneur, CEO, professional athlete, or simply someone who seeks to get more out of everyday life. They are laws so they will always work as long as you are in harmony with them.

Ralph Waldo Emerson once said, *"There is no planet, sun, or star that could hold you, if you but knew what you are."*

Be A Beast goes a long way in showing you who you are and what you are really capable of.

– **Bob Proctor**, bestselling author of *You Were Born Rich*

Preface

When I was young, my father was a chaplain in the Navy, so we moved about every two to three years. I remember being in 5th grade and being pretty good in every sport I played. We lived in Fullerton, California at the time. The coaches said I was fast, and I was fast—running for touchdown after touchdown. They told me I had good hands, and I had good hands—catching pass after pass.

We then moved to North Carolina and I remember my football coach in his strong sergeant–like voice telling me, "Austin, you are slow as molasses." Huh? What happened to being fast? Well, I didn't know any better, so I believed him—and sure enough, I became slow as molasses.

I began to look at myself differently, and also gained a bunch of extra weight. How could this "golden boy" from Southern California no longer be fast or a star athlete? Why was I now looking over my shoulder as I ran the ball, wondering if someone was going to catch me?

How did I so quickly become just an average athlete that was becoming fat almost overnight? No longer was I the quarterback or receiver, now they put me on the defensive line, where the "bigger" boys played.

After two and a half years in North Carolina, lucky for me, my dad got transferred again—this time to Hawaii. The first day at football practice I overheard the coaches saying that this new kid (me) was kind of quick. I thought to myself, "Thank God!! Somehow, I'm quick again!"

That's all I needed to hear. I picked up the pace and ran for touchdown after touchdown again—and what also happened was I naturally shed the extra weight to be the athlete I once was back in Southern California.

This became a great passion of mine—discovering what effects the opinions of others had on me. Later, as I received college scholarships in both football and baseball, it became my driving-force to find out why in certain environments I was a star athlete and in others I wasn't (and how even my body changed to fit my self-image).

The reason I decided to major in psychology and physical education was to be a great coach, and I knew firsthand the *power* they had on one's life—both good and bad. So as someone in that sort of position, I wanted to be sure that I was a *positive* influence on every athlete.

When a tragic car accident almost killed me while I was still in college, I decided to switch to tennis to rehabilitate myself—and learned to walk and run again. After a lot of hard work and playing catch-up, I went on to gain a world ranking in professional tennis and had a chance to travel the globe. This is where my "laboratory" work truly started, and where my "12-Step BE A BEAST Process" began to take form.

The events of our lives shape us and mold us into who we become as both athletes and adults. And, as you can see through these personal experiences and my history, the "why" of this BE A BEAST book becomes very obvious.

As a young person growing up, I let others tell me who I was or who I wasn't. This book and my lifework come together to help you know who you really are. It will help encourage you to open up to your own greatness.

Just keep in mind that habits are formed by practice. For example, if you continue to practice the wrong swing in golf, it will remain a bad swing and wrong technique. It is my intention that this book provides you with a practice to follow, where there is no other result than a perfect swing.

That is precisely why Roger and I became partners—to combine our coaching techniques and create this powerful "mental mindset" training. I am so grateful we did—and as fate would have it, just in the nick of time for sure!

Introduction

A Journey Of Transformation

Each and every one of us has a life purpose and nothing ever happens by chance or coincidence. Knowing this, it is important to realize that every circumstance and situation has a purpose imbedded in it towards the fulfillment of our life's work. Very few people, however, discover and live according to their mission and reason for being. As a result, they use little of their true potential.

Over generations of time we have gradually become, and alarmingly so, unaware of who we really are and what we are truly capable of. Our true potential lies dormant deep within the subterranean realms of our lives, yearning to be released in order to serve us. But by answering the call, the world inevitably becomes a better place to live. Though first we must learn to unleash this potential.

While these existing conditions are of great concern, likewise, there are also exciting times ahead and optimistic viewpoints about our future to embrace. There is no doubt that we are living in the dawn of an awakening, where knowledge is pouring in on us at a rate unprecedented in the history of mankind.

For avid seekers of truth who, through humility, remain open and willing to further advance in the quest for self-mastery, hidden mysteries will be unveiled. And in doing so, we will undoubtedly discover more about "who we really are" and "what we are truly capable of." Again, these are truly exciting times.

Warriors, Not Worriers

Problems Are Opportunities In Disguise

"Each of us has a mission and purpose that can only be unveiled by experiencing trials, extracting the good from them, and moving onto the next moment of our lives with gratitude for the lessons learned!"

– Roger Anthony

Life is so beautifully designed for us to learn from all of our experiences on a continual basis. And, it just so happens that our greatest growth comes through our greatest challenges. As such, each of us has a mission and purpose that can only be unveiled by experiencing trials, extracting the good from them, and moving onto the next moment of our lives with gratitude for the lessons learned.

Every experience unveils a little more about who we really are, what we are capable of, where we are meant to be going, and how we are going to get there. In light of this understanding, we see that problems aren't problems; they are opportunities in disguise. They are challenges designed to build within us the attributes that make up strength of character and lead us to discover and fulfill our true reason for being.

When confronted with a problem, a warrior sees it for what it really is—a challenge. A warrior remains relaxed, overcomes the challenge, learns from it, and moves forward. The trick here is to be more of a warrior and less of a worrier—the choice is yours!

Winning Habits

More Than 65,000 Thoughts Per Day...

"These unique training methods enable us to see what makes one person succeed and why another one fails."

– Dave Austin

Did you know we each have over 65,000 thoughts a day? And, many of these thoughts distract us from the important things needed to accomplish our goals.

When adversity, pressure, or nerves hit, most of us let negative thoughts control the situation—if we have not had the proper training to do otherwise. We stuff these nerves rather than using them to fuel our desires.

When we follow a very simple "12-Step BE A BEAST Process," we *light the fire from the inside out*, rather than letting the outer circumstances control our lives. To become a champion in anything, it takes practice and repetition. We are going to give you some practical steps to incorporate into your daily life that create winning habits and new thought patterns.

It's a proven process that gets you from where you currently are, to where you ultimately want to be. By using this step-by-step process, you will discover how belief systems shape your life, and how just about everything revolves around "what we believe to be true" about our environment and ourselves.

Based on the principles I've developed during years of mental performance coaching for professional athletes and corporate clients, we'll present proven methods of how to stay "in the zone" and at the top of your profession. We then tie it all together with Roger's proven "Memory Anchor System" that incorporates "animal instincts" to guide you on this journey. And, trust me when I say—the power of the beast works!

What's a BEAST Principle?

It is a unique way to "tap into your animal instincts" and achieve "extreme focus" in all you do. It is your fully loaded toolkit to help "get your mind working *for* you rather than against you." It gets your thoughts and actions to work for you in any situation.

So often, we just *react* to situations and conditional habits that don't necessarily serve us very well. Every one of the BE A BEAST "mental mindset" steps in this innovative program has proven to work at the highest level of pressure zones and is triggered by one word that represents an animal instinct principle. Each words is packed with powerful meanings that make it easy to access the lessons in a millisecond.

And very often, we only have a millisecond to respond to a situation or crisis—so it's easy to be distracted by negative thoughts. The BE A BEAST principles show us how to "shift" into more supportive mental mindset thoughts instantly, knowing that once you change your mindset, your life will change forever.

Simply stated, the best description or definition for BE A BEAST is—performance driven results;

* It's the culmination of more than 30 years of mental mindset principles in action with pro sports teams and individual athletes, that raised their games to heights that included winning the pennant and competing in world championships;

* And, it's the blend of specialized mental retention principles, combined with more than 30 years of corporate sales training that utilizes a unique "memory recall system" that boasts an amazing 92% retention rate—and applies to everything.

In other words, we've taken the #1 proven and tested training and retention program created by Roger Anthony—a system where you're not just inspired, but where you're able to instantly recall high performance concepts through the use of one word triggers—and combine that with the Extreme Focus 12-step "mental mindset" process—which is proven to win at every level in high-level sports competition. By doing so, you have a "winning formula." One that is certainly effective enough to unleash the champion from within.

How This Applies To You

Changing Your World From The Inside Out
"A proven process that moves you from where you are, to where you ultimately want to be...in the zone."

– Dave Austin

To truly succeed at every level of life, you must be awake to your own habitual patterns, and shift into conscious living. This is where you will have clearer vision and start living *into* your dreams, rather than being too busy to achieve them.

24

In fact, you need to "slow down to get there fast." Then, once you begin to follow the animal guides and transformative principles that are laid out here for you, time will begin to "stand still" for your every demand.

Most knew that Roger was a master teacher. But what many did not know is that he was also a world-class athlete himself. It would be a safe bet to say there was no other person on this planet who could do what Roger did with the speed-bag. In fact, in that sport he was a world-champion athlete—no one could compete with him on that bag. He was at a mastery level and took his level of focus to an entirely new level.

Likewise, these mindset techniques take leadership to a new level of focus, and is unlike any other training. Both Roger and I have been leaders in this arena, and have guided Fortune 500 companies to amazing results and unparalleled championship results in the process.

Why do some fail when others succeed?

You are in for a treat, because the synergy from blending two very successful programs together has created a highly effective road map for you to follow in order to achieve your desired successes. And, this unique training method will enable you to take your life to the highest level imaginable.

This will change your world from the "inside out" with easy to remember animal guides. It's one thing to learn something, but another to become so thoroughly entrenched in it that you can use it in order to handle every situation you come up against—as there is an answer to *every* question within these animals.

We are going to give you a "behind the scenes" look at these effective training methods to see what makes one person succeed and why another one fails. And, an opportunity to put these winning habits and skill sets into practice for performance driven results.

Why Listen To Us?

#1 In Retention Plus Championship Results

"We use the 'animal world' to help guide us along our pathway to achieve dynamic success. And, it is in drilling through the crust of negative conditioning, with the diamond tip of a positive attitude, that we discover a reservoir of personal power that is available and on call to handle any situation"

– Roger M. Anthony

What benefit will you get from studying the somewhat unorthodox methods we use in BE A BEAST? In other words, why listen to us? The answer is because we combine a proven winning formula from the athletic fields and anchor those steps with the #1 proven retention program created to expand this success into the workplace. That's a powerful combination.

These are methodologies that have worked absolute miracles on both the athletic fields as well as within corporate boardrooms. I may be biased, but it is my opinion that no other leadership book has been written with a retention level built-in that is as effective as the "Memory Anchor System" we have incorporated.

Studies show, that when we hear something for the first time, we tend to forget 50% immediately—and just two days later we've already forgotten 75%, and a week later we've forgotten most all of it! Obviously, there is a lot of room for improvement here.

Even in the very best trainings, without looking at notes, people only recall on average about 14%-15%. Yet, with Roger's "Memory Anchor System," the average class recall is an unprecedented 92%!

This means almost 100% of its students are able to remember and apply the principles when they need them the most. And, that is when they have left the training room and are back in the field of life!

"Tap into your true instincts. That is when you allow yourself to play at the highest level and succeed."

– Dave Austin

September 30, 2012

Carolina Panthers vs. the undefeated Atlanta Falcons.

Fourth quarter. Down by three.

3rd and 10 at Atlanta's own 36-yard line.

The play is called; a screen pass to Kealoha Pilares #81.

A two-minute timeout is called.

The game is on the line. Carolina must get those 10 yards.

Quarterback Cam Newton drops back...

Kealoha Pilares shifts into beast mode—RESPA™

RELAX

Break huddle. Take a deep breath.

EVALUATE

Scan field. Visualize play.

STRATEGIZE

Align left. See the ball.

PATIENCE

Make catch. Scan the defenders.

ACT

Burst into 5th gear. Run 36 yards.

Touchdown!! The crocodile survives another day.

"Crocodiles roamed the Earth with the dinosaurs; sharing hunting grounds and experiencing the same rapidly changing environment. There are 23 species of crocodilians thriving today. But, when was the last time you saw a dinosaur?"

– Roger M. Anthony

"The difference between winning and losing many times is just mere inches. Be A Beast supplies you with those inches and a whole lot more. Utilize these sound principles to become a champion in your own life."

What's "Be A Beast?"

BE A BEAST is just that—a defining moment when the game is on the line, and the difference between winning and losing is only a matter of inches. Being "a beast" is when your opportunity to rise or fall is at hand, and you utilize everything you've got to rise up!

To illustrate this point, let's use the following speech given by Al Pacino in the movie, *Any Given Sunday*:

> *Life is just a game of inches. So is football.*
> *Because in either game, life or football,*
> *the margin for error is so small.*
>
> *One half step too late or too early,*
> *you don't quite make it.*
> *One half second too slow or too fast,*
> *and you don't quite catch it.*
>
> *The inches we need are everywhere around us.*
> *They are in every break of the game,*
> *every minute, every second.*
>
> *On this team, we fight for that inch.*
> *On this team, we tear ourselves,*
> *and everyone around us to pieces for that inch.*
>
> *We CLAW with our fingernails for that inch.*
> *Cause we know, when we add up all those inches*
> *that's going to make the...difference*
> *between WINNING and LOSING*
>
> *Between LIVING and DYING.*

Kealoha Pilares, receiver for the Carolina Panthers, was fully aware of those inches. He knew the actual difference they make in winning and losing, and he was willing to do whatever it took to get those inches to help his team.

29

He had put in the time, and the training, in preparation of that moment when his team needed him to deliver results. Kealoha Pilares had the advantage with his "winning mental mindset" training. He had already done his prep.

Welcome To BE A BEAST

Tapping Back Into Your Animal Instincts

"These 'animal guides' will give you a sense of freedom that you have not yet had before."

– Dave Austin

We all have "a beast" within us, and yet, there are times when the power of our mind keeps it from being unleashed. But, when we tap into our true instinctive nature, that's when we allow ourselves to play at the highest level. And, it does not matter if you are a professional athlete, or a CEO, or an entrepreneur—or simply someone who seeks to get more out of everyday life. The principles are the same.

This specialized training came into existence partially as a gift from God, partially through many trials and tribulations, and mainly through the deep love and respect I have for my partner and eternal friend, Roger Anthony. We had met years earlier, and in those first moments together, we both knew to the core of our beings that our life mission and purpose had just collided—but in a very, very good way.

Over the years, our paths crossed time and time again, as we got to know each other at a deep and spiritual level. We hosted personal development trainings as a team, traveled to film on the Great Wall of China and at the Taj Mahal, and also had the great privilege of speaking at the World's Wellness Women's Congress in Chennai, India along with Bob Proctor—where 50+ countries and world delegations were represented

So again, welcome to taking a peek into a world that utilizes "beasts" as teachers and guides to up-level your life and careers. This at first may seem unusual and a bit unconventional, but believe me, soon enough they'll be some of your favorite companions.

30

Awaken To Our True Nature

One of the things we're going to do here is explore my 12-step "mental mindset" process. And, in doing so, we are going to anchor each of these steps with a different animal that will be a "mental trigger anchor" to help remind us when we start to slide into "Oh, my gosh, I've got to make this sale." Or, "I've got to win this point," or whatever.

By utilizing these principles, you'll be able to tap back into your animal instincts—behaviors that are going to work for you in whatever circumstances you may face. These "animal guides" are going to give you a sense of freedom that you have not yet had before. They are going to allow you to excel freely, and play the game with ease—no matter what game that may be.

We will tie an animal companion into each teaching principle who will assist in keeping you "awake" to your true nature and greatest potential. The names of each of these animal guides are the "mental triggers" that will shift you back on track instantly, especially when you wander into "conditional thinking."

Meet Our Overseeing Guides

Scaling The Peaks Of Integrity And Patience

"Personal mastery is living in harmony with one's created design, and being anchored in integrity."

– Roger M. Anthony

In addition to the twelve BE A BEAST animal companions, we have three more that'll be our "overseeing guides;" RESPA and INROCK, the two that are described below, and a third one, COUR, that will be discussed in the closing chapter of this book.

So get ready—because within these pages you'll learn exactly how to, quickly and easily, apply these animal instinct principles into your life—and on a daily basis, turn all obstacles into opportunities. It is through the regular practice and use of these BE A BEAST mental triggers that you will shift your life into right action.

I didn't become a professional tennis player by just "knowing" how to play tennis. I had to practice my strokes over and over—and use what I had learned by putting that knowledge into action. It takes consistent focus and dedication. And after awhile, my new habits began *working for me rather than against me.*

Let the animal instinct principles presented here serve not only as a valuable and unique road map to your intended destination, but also as a guide to keep you steadfast on your path. And, be sure to always enjoy the journey—as it's a process, so enjoy!

We all have the beast instincts within us

The gift of anchoring the 12-step "mental mindset" process with the animal kingdom is so when you're on the field of battle, and it's very intense with pressure, you can tap into those instincts and *be* that beast.

Rather than being bogged down by our own limitations getting in the way with thoughts like, "What about this? What about that?" let's be more like a crocodile who doesn't worry about making a mistake. The crocodile simply goes out and does it's thing.

And so, by quieting your mind chatter and using your instincts more, you can achieve greater focus. This will be as invaluable for you, as it is with my clients and athletes. Many times when I work with athletes, we use just "one word" as a trigger to shift their focus. That is all we need. Lucky for us, we have more than one word to draw upon—since we have fifteen animal principles here to work with.

These anchoring success principles will literally help us remember what we need to do and when we need it the most—whether we're in the heat of the battle, or in the battlefield of our everyday lives

Now, without diving into the 12-step process just yet, let's anchor the first concepts right now; with RESPA and INROCK. These first two overseeing guides are the ones that I personally use all the time—and are so powerful they will travel with us throughout each of these subsequent 12-steps.

RESPA™ (The Crocodile)

Personal Control Through Self-Discipline

"RESPA your way through life."

– Roger M. Anthony

This is the personal mastery system for developing self-discipline, maintaining composure, and personal control in one's life. It's the backbone upon which integrity, enlightenment, and personal control are developed and maintained.

Relax :: enhances creativity, restores energy.

Evaluate :: determine current reality.

Strategize :: layout an action plan.

Patience :: re-evaluate and adjust if necessary.

Act :: simply do it and move with focused action.

RESPA is a great way to experience personal control through self-mastery; it enhances creativity and opens the door to our personal power and potential.

Adapting to a changing environment

The first creature that we use is a true beast—I mean it really is the beast of all beasts. It's the crocodile. Did you know the crocodile outlived the dinosaur? It's interesting to note, that the crocodile roamed the Earth alongside its cousins, the dinosaurs. And, I mean this literally, the crocodiles and dinosaurs are cousins.

They do look very much alike. When you see various species of dinosaurs and crocodiles, there's no doubt about it, the crocodile is a dinosaur of a sort. But, crocodiles had something that was different—and as it turned out that something was invaluable to its very survival. It had the innate ability to adapt in a changing environment. The crocodile had adaptability.

A capacity to remain flexible in order to thrive

During the pre-historic ages, the crocodile roamed the Earth with its cousins the dinosaurs side-by-side. They both shared the same environment and had the same resources available to them in order to survive—and here's the big key, they both experienced the same dynamically changing environment around them.

They shared the same hunting grounds, experienced the same changing environment—however, today there are 23 species of crocodilians alive. And, by the way, not just alive but thriving. When was the last time you or I ever saw a dinosaur alive? Exactly!

This is precisely why we chose the crocodile as one of our overseeing guides—because they demonstrate such a great capacity to be incredibly flexible—whereas the dinosaur wasn't. The crocodile was able to adapt and be flexible in a dynamically changing environment.

Let's take this same concept into the sports world. What happens on the field when something goes wrong and we find ourselves fallen flat on our face? If we are able to keep our laser, or in most cases, our extreme focus where it needs to be, and be flexible in that moment, we get back up and keep going. And, when we do get up, they had better move out of the way, because we've learned from that experience and are going to adapt.

A strategic methodology for survival

And so, our first overseeing guide is a crocodile, and his name is RESPA. That's R-E-S-P-A. The reason for this is that crocodiles are renowned for their strategic planning system and methodology of surviving. For instance, the first thing they do when they are under extreme pressure is to *relax*.

You see, in a relaxed state, as human beings, we are far better able to think more clearly and to move more quickly. Therefore, the first thing we must do is to relax—that's the "R" in R-E-S-P-A. Now, the second thing we must do, when facing a pressure situation—or any situation for that matter—is to "E" *evaluate* the situation. This brings me to an important thing to point out about my partner, Roger Anthony.

Roger was always appreciated for one, his Australian accent—although he said we American's were "cheeky buggers," and the one's who talked funny—but two, for his references to being "hoodwinked" in all manner of things. It always amazed him how often human beings were hoodwinked about what was actually real and what was more of an illusion than fact.

The first thing we must do is...relax

When we are in a relaxed state, we are then in a much better place to be able to evaluate the situation—and see things creatively for how they really are, and not for how our mind hoodwinks us into seeing them to be, when we're uptight, stressed, worried, or anxious.

When we're in a relaxed state, we are also better able to control any unforeseen circumstance or situation. Relax, Evaluate and then we lay out an "S" for *strategy*—which is how we're going to be moving through all of this. So Relax, Evaluate, lay out our Strategy, and then we have "P" which is the *patience* to re-evaluate just for a nano second—and then "A" is when we *act*. So, this crocodile named RESPA teaches us that in all circumstances and situations, a master chooses to *Relax*, *Evaluate*, lay out a *Strategy*, have *Patience* and then *Act*.

That is the principle of R-E-S-P-A. And, to me this is just so amazing. I have had some NFL football players and Major League baseball players who "go off" in a good way while using RESPA. They would just have a great outing, and I'd call them afterwards to debrief, and they'd say, "RESPA, all I did was RESPA'd."

I even once had a race car driver who said, "I used BRESPA" to win the race. And, by that he meant that he also used his *breathe*—you know, he just added his own little "B" to the front of it. This is because right before the race we talked about his breathing, and how it can be so important.

So, RESPA becomes such a great concept. Because if you can see yourself playing in that state of mind we've just described, and you "become that" principle, then you are free to be a champion—and the game changer you're looking to be.

The eye of the crocodile

One more thing while we're talking about our friend the crocodile is that while a crocodile is in murky water, they actually close their second eyelid. It's like wearing a pair of goggles, only it's a little bit better than those goggles we use while swimming because when they close that second eyelid, they can actually see through the muck and muddy stream.

So when we're on the playing field in life, and we've got the eye of a crocodile, we simply close that second eyelid and we can see things for how they really are. To me, that's like describing Wayne Gretsky when he was playing professional hockey. He saw things before others did. He didn't move to where the puck was—he moved to where the puck was *going* to be. It seems that "The Great One" must have had crocodile eyelids.

The same thing with Michael Jordan or Magic Johnson in basketball. You know they saw things that others didn't—as a fan you watch and they throw a pass to what looks like no one, and you're like, "what?" and then there's a guy there to catch it, as if by magic. That is the principle of RESPA all the way.

How exactly do I use RESPA, when I am feeling the pressure?

It's like learning any new skill—you practice. I could never have been a professional tennis player without practicing, or without hitting thousands of tennis balls, in order to not even have to think about the mechanics of the game—it became automatic. A habit is formed by repetition. So if every morning you got up and took a deep breath, and repeated the principle of RESPA in your mind or by saying it out loud, your mind would begin to get familiar with that word, and begin to automatically relax through this mental trigger. And, in a relaxed state of mind, it is easier to make smart decisions.

It's all about anticipation. Which reminds me of a professional baseball client of mine and actually all of my athlete clients—such great crocodiles they are. Many times this one MLB player in particular tells me just how much he appreciates these principles, and how important the crocodile has been for him. He has learned well how powerful it is to use RESPA in all circumstances and situations—especially in pitching.

36

So now, in the future, when pressure situations come up, you can simply say "RESPA" and your body will respond by relaxing first—and before your emotions are able to take you away from a clear smart decision.

I have seen an entire culture of a company change by this simple practice. Once they learned the principle of RESPA, everyone began to work together as a team, and as a result the company took off and became much stronger overall. Not to mention that great innovation and creative things are born out of a relaxed state of mind. It is definitely what I would call a "winning habit" and one that would greatly benefit all.

Set your intentions and choose your path

When you use the RESPA principle on a regular basis, life becomes effortless—and what you see in your mind in advance, literally seems to fall right into your lap. For example, recently I had driven out to the MLB Spring Training camp in Arizona to meet with the manager of one of the baseball teams.

This was a six and a half hour drive for me from San Diego to Scottsdale. I ended up getting to my hotel fairly late in the evening, but was up early and prepared for our 7:45 a.m. meeting the next morning. One of the first things I did was to set my 3 intentions and then I gave myself a visualization to get locked in.

When I arrived at the training facility, the main lobby was locked and no one was there. So, I talked my way around to the back of the facility and got in through that entrance. From there I went to the team manager's office and walked right into a meeting that was going on. Feeling the awkwardness of the situation, I quickly excused myself and went out to an empty lobby to wait. What was happening here? Did I get the time mixed up? Had I been stood up?

I figured there were a couple of options here. One, I could leave in anger and probably never expect to hear from this ball club again. Or, the other option was to practice the principle of RESPA. This is the route I chose to take—and it's one I'd recommend you also take if you find yourself in a similar situation. In that moment of RESPA, I allowed myself to be able to tap back into gratitude for even having this opportunity.

Seriously, how many people are given the chance to do the work I do? I have to admit, and even after all these years, I feel like a kid in a candy store being able to do what I do. Tapping back into this, I then put my entire focus on staying in that feeling of gratitude.

During this RESPA time, I thought about what was the outcome that I desired—and continued to sit there for a moment to just breathe into those feelings. I tapped into knowing I was in the right place, and that the perfect situation would just show up. As I continued to wait, I used my time wisely and in fact made some edits to this book—something I probably would not have had the time to do otherwise. I was pleased with myself for making what easily could have been a "poor me" moment into a productive one.

How long should I use the RESPA principle?

Well that depends on the situation and what is required. You can go through the process in a nano second, or you can stay a little longer in the patience part—and take the time required to find the best outcome. For example, if I get a letter or email that gets me angry or upset, I will take at least 24 hours to RESPA before I reply. I may draft up my response, but I never hit the "send" button until I have allowed the process of RESPA to help me see the situation from a clear and calm state of mind. This gives me a chance to come from a stronger point of view, or from a perspective after the emotions have simmered down—and when I have more patience. There have been many times when I look at the same correspondence the next day or later on, and it no longer hits me as hard. This is when I am better able to find a calm strength in order to draft a much better and more productive reply.

An hour and a half later at this spring training opportunity, the perfect time did show up for me. I'd originally wanted to meet with not just the manager, but also with two of his coaches who I also enjoyed spending time with—even though each had texted me earlier saying they were not going to be available.

But, in my RESPA time, I saw myself sitting there with all three in the managers office. One and a half hours later, that is exactly what was taking place.

What are the chances of that? I don't know, but I do know I could have held on to a smoldering anger and a "poor me" attitude—which probably would not have put me in the position to realize my intentions. But, RESPA brought me back to higher ground as did the next principle of INROCK which has to do with integrity. All in all, the meeting ended up being productive and the "championship journey" continues.

So, if we are to recap the principle of RESPA, it is a way to experience personal self-control through self-mastery. It is something you want to use at the start of your day, and when you begin any project. It is a great habit to develop for every area of your life.

When you integrate RESPA into your daily habits, it increases awareness and personal stability. It can also increase your creativity, and open the door to your personal power and potential. Again, it's the backbone upon which integrity, enlightenment, and personal control are developed and maintained.

Attain Personal Control: Through Self-Mastery

It's time to adopt a system for maintaining composure, self-discipline and personal control...

Implementation Checklist +Results:

* Use at the beginning of each day.
* Use at the start of projects.
* Develop as a habit for all areas of life.

RESPA your way through life—as it greatly increases and enhances your awareness, inspiration, integrity, personal stability, creativity, and also opens the door to your personal power and potential.

" In the development of wisdom,
one must gather the firewood of
knowledge, and ignite it by striking
the flint of courage against the rock
of self-discipline, thus creating
fires of understanding. Wisdom,
therefore, is knowledge on fire."

INROCK™ (The Eagle)

Integrity Is The Rock

*"It is living in harmony with one's created design,
anchored at all times to a solid foundation."*

– Roger M. Anthony

Integrity is the rock and represents the principle of INROCK. It is a sure foundation for our personal and business lives, and means being *receiver of correct knowledge*, instead of receivers of *falseness appearing real*. The integrity of INROCK is the universal master principle of completeness, oneness, wholeness, and reliability, anchored to principles of truth.

So, now that we've received an overseeing animal guide that covers the ground and murky waters, how about one from high above? Which animal do you think is going to give us a higher perspective from the air, so that we have both vantage points covered?

Living in accordance with integrity

Well, this one is a bald eagle and the reason we use a bald eagle—whose name by the way is INROCK and we'll get to what that name means in a minute—is because an eagle is renowned for its ability to use the wind currents of nature. They don't fight it. They go in the flow. They don't get stressed about things, and they enjoy the moment and the journey.

I've used this principle a lot in my coaching work and especially when I am doing a "game ready" with my athlete clients. Many times, when using a visualization technique, I utilize the eagle, and each time I think, "Wow, this is incredible!" Because, one of the things I always say is to enjoy the process—which an eagle certainly does.

You know, if it's a missed hit or you foul up a little bit, learn from it, but enjoy that moment and get back up again. In doing so, you're in a better space to improve when you can have that kind of attitude.

Using the currents of nature

As said before, the eagle uses the wind currents, or the thermal currents in nature to their advantage. They also have incredible vision, because they're always relaxed. You watch an eagle flying, and can see that it's very graceful, very powerful, has great vision, and can see 8x's more powerfully than a human being can.

Again, while they're flying about, they're using the natural wind currents of Mother Nature. And so, they never get frazzled. They're never exhausted. Have you ever seen an eagle plummet out of the sky out of exhaustion? No, I've never seen it happen.

And it's because they're not worried, or stressed, or flapping their wings and getting all out of control. An eagle teaches us the art of living in accordance with integrity. And, I see the wind currents and the thermal currents of our lives to be the thermal currents of integrity. That's the key.

If you commit to somebody that you're going to do something, whether it's your coach or your trainer, or yourself or your parents, it doesn't matter—the key is stick by your word. Be a person of integrity. And, if you're saying you're going out there to win, then go out there and make sure you live in integrity—and then you're going to win. That's all there is to it.

Rise above the pecking crows

So again, the name of the eagle is INROCK and it stands for integrity, that's the "IN" part; and "ROCK," which represents it's on a solid foundation—in other words, integrity is the rock.

Another aspect of INROCK and one thing I love about the eagle is they have a larger lung capacity than other birds. So when the crows come and claw at their feet, or peck at their feet, instead of it pecking right back at them, the eagle just spreads it wings and rises above.

42

The crow tries to go up that high in pursuit, but it can't breathe up there. So I like to use INROCK when you're in a situation, and you need to just be the eagle. Rise up above it. Lift up above it. By using integrity as the rock, you've got the capacity that others don't.

That's exactly how it works. And the big thing about just rising above is it uses very little energy. Why would an eagle waste energy trying to attack a crow, when it can just make one flick of its wings and it goes up higher and out of their reach?

That's all there is to it. It's all about mind power and control, right? I love this and gave that principle to a football receiver one time who had this cornerback that was just pestering him on and on—giving him all kinds of trouble. The cornerback in this moment was the crow. And, instead of buying into all that stuff, all the receiver did was rise above it. This of course only bugged the cornerback more—seeing as how it hadn't bothered this receiver. My client was like, "You know, so what? I've got my job to do, so forget this guy."

He then made a quick cut across the field and won the game by taking it into the end zone. He went, "You know I don't need to peck with you, I'll just fly above you." By doing that, he was in his own kind of zone.

Fly with the eagles

One time I was brought in to work with the executive team of an established shipping company. They all got along pretty well on the surface, but there was an undercurrent where they pecked like crows rather than lift each other up to new heights.

As we went through a process and I gave them the opportunity to "check their egos at the front door," the leaders took on a newfound strength and the invisible walls began to fall. The corporation began to soar, just like the eagle that lifts his wings to rise above the pecking crows. Each executive became an eagle themselves, and the culture of the company shifted. Each department began to work together as a team, instead of continuing to compete with one another. When this happens, the company's revenues can go up and moral can take flight.

In every situation when you choose to soar with the eagles instead of pecking with crows, everyone is lifted to new heights.

Why does integrity play such a big role in being successful?

When you are out of integrity with yourself, you lack in self-esteem. With low self-esteem, it is harder for you to achieve greatness. Your "trust muscle" in yourself gets chipped away. And, the next time you need to step it up and perform, your subconscious sabotages any chances of victory. One of the biggest advantages of living in integrity is, not only will you have a higher self-image, but life is less stressful. When others know they can count on your word—life is easier and your business will flourish.

Years ago, I learned a valuable lesson about the real value of people knowing your word is golden. I was having lunch after playing tennis with recording artist, Kenny Rogers, at his home. He was an avid tennis player and would play in the morning, then fly off in his private jet to a concert that night. A nice lifestyle.

One day, after Kenny had jetted off somewhere, I was talking to his manager, Ken Kragen—who at the time also managed Lionel Richie. I asked Ken, "What's the key to success?" I will never forget what he said next, "That people know my word is my word."

He went on to tell about a time when Kenny had asked him if he had made a call he was suppose to make, it would have been easy to say "Yes, but I haven't heard back from them yet." Ken had made a decision early on to never cross that line. One small white lie would lower the standards he'd set for himself.

You are important enough to be honest with

We often forget that even if no one else knows, *we know* when we have been not so honest, or have bent the truth. Let me ask you this—aren't YOU important enough to always be honest with yourself?

We chip away at our own "trust muscles," and whether we know it or not, this creates a lowered self-esteem. And, low self-esteem makes it nearly impossible to have sustaining and long-term success.

44

Years later, while being a consultant for a company, I had an opportunity to put together a multi-million dollar deal for them. Everything was going great, until all of a sudden the buyer looked at me and asked a question that I hadn't thought of beforehand. Right as I was about to come up with some kind of "winging it answer" to try and get by without blowing this major deal, I remembered Ken's advice.

So instead, I simply said, "That's a great question that I don't know the answer to. But, I will research it and within 24 hours I will have an answer for you." At that moment I thought I had killed the deal. It is in my nature to feel that I should have all the answers to just about anything—but this time I basically put RESPA into action and paused, which helped me stay in the principle of INROCK. The buyer then told me if I got that answer for him, that he would do the deal. He also said he had more faith in the project, because I didn't try to B.S. him like so many others try to do. Thanks to Ken, as I would have blown the deal if I didn't go to the highest level of integrity within that moment.

Being in integrity with your word

That was the beauty of knowing Roger Anthony—you could always count on his word. In the past, I might have tried to avoid a sticky situation hoping it might go away, but Roger would pull me aside to say, "Let's have an 'integ' moment (which simply meant we needed to address the situation with the highest of integrity and respect). So even if I had done something which he didn't agree with, it would never fester since we would always get it out and on the table to discuss.

And, by doing this, we both had the opportunity to grow from the experience. Having the highest level of integrity is not stuffing things, but sharing openly and honestly when someone has let you down or has done something that you are not completely comfortable with. This practice INROCK simply holds everyone to a higher level of accountability.

Remember, this is not done like in a "crow-pecking" way. Instead, when you have trust in each other and you come from the eagle's higher elevation and point of view, small matters are handled with ease before they become bigger obstacles to navigate.

A good practice to do to strengthen your INROCK muscles is to "Accept who I was, love who I am, and be excited about who I am becoming." Always be honest with yourself, about self, to self, and to others.

What if someone I care about hurts me by their actions?

Living in full integrity means being honest with that person and letting them know exactly how their actions have affected you. Try not to respond in anger and don't hold it in, or hold on to it. Just come from a place that it is apparent you care enough about this person to share your feelings with them—and how in the future you would like to see something different occur. Always come from the point of view of being open and honest, and try to leave hurt emotions or angst out of the equations. And, if you practice RESPA beforehand, it will most assuredly go more smoothly and be received in a much more honest manner.

So, if we are to recap the principle of INROCK, it is about achieving relationship integrity through personal integrity. It greatly assists in developing a sense of personal freedom. It encourages others to be honest with you and builds up trust and respect.

Living in full integrity is not just "never lying," but being bold enough to live your word and in truth. It creates unity, wholeness, and moral soundness—and builds up your self-esteem. Remove the false facades and follow through on your commitments.

Achieve Relationship Integrity: Through Personal Integrity

It's time to be receivers of correct knowledge, rather than receivers of falseness appearing real...

Implementation Checklist +Results:

* Be honest about self - to yourself and to others.
* Remove false facades.
* Follow through on commitments.
* Accept who I was, love who I am, be excited about who I am becoming.

What does this principle provide? It greatly assists in developing a sense of personal freedom, encourages others to be honest with you, builds trust and respect, and creates unity, wholeness and moral soundness. It also develops self-awareness, a positive attitude, and thus assertiveness skills.

Part I

Setting Your Course

What you feed will grow…what you starve will die. So, be sure to feed yourself with a daily dose of positive thoughts!

Our minds are an important asset. They will either work for us or against us. But, how do we truly get our minds to work for us in an ever-changing world that seems to be moving faster and faster, and keeps us off-balance and in chaos? How do we break free from the chains that bind us and want to pull us back to our familiar conditional thinking in order to expand and grow into a grander and better version of ourselves each and everyday? The answer is you set your course and turn obstacles into opportunities by using very specific "mental mindset" triggers to snap you back into right action.

"I am forever amazed at the unlimited power of my subconscious mind for positive or negative, and yet, I stand in wonder at how simply I choose its governing influence upon my life through the gateway of the conscious mind."

Chapter 1

MIMA & LIMA™ (The Armadillos)

In This Chapter

* Learning how beliefs are related to what shows up in life
* Taking a look at your core beliefs and if they support you or not
* Seeing how mind mastery equates to life mastery

"While working with Dave, I ended up leading my team in both home runs (30) and RBI's (90)..."

– Jason Kubel, LF, Arizona DiamondBacks

You don't need a doctorate degree in psychiatry to know whether you've allowed your mind to keep you stuck in familiar patterns. Take a look at your current life and more importantly, your *results* to see if your ability to achieve your greatest desires are being held prisoner within a cage—when all along you have the key to your own everlasting freedom.

An important thing to be aware of is that a negative habit is contained in a seed so small as to appear harmless. Once allowed to be sown however, it grows unnoticeable until it is a vine that viciously entwines and ensnares. For the sake of personal freedom, we are obligated to watchfully stand guard, and immediately remove any seed of influence that would eventually lead to the mental, physical, or spiritual imprisonment of our soul.

Beliefs Create Your Reality

Have you ever thought about what is at the core of your belief structures and at the foundation on which your actions are built upon? This is very important and where it all really begins—where the rubber meets the road. By understanding what is, and what is not serving you, we can discard any beliefs that no longer provide a purpose—we can build strength upon those beliefs that support our goals and aspirations.

In this chapter, we will begin to explore the "12-Step BE A BEAST Process" as we dive deep underneath the layers of our subconscious mind in order to focus on, and strengthen, our core beliefs—as well as where we discover the meaning of what I say often, "Champions are champions *before* they are champions."

Core Structures

Beliefs and Mental Performance

"Every decision in your life is controlled by your beliefs and values. You may not realize it, but you have the power to choose what you believe about your life, people, money and health. You can either choose beliefs that limit you, or beliefs that empower you to move toward success. Your beliefs energize you to create the world you want to live in right now. The key is to be aware of them because what you value determines what you focus on."

– Tony Robbins

Step One is all about your core beliefs and how to use your belief systems to shape your individual reality and life experiences. This is one of the biggest keys that I have found while working in sports and from playing as a professional athlete myself.

How deep down do you really believe? At what level do you cave in? Do you truly trust in yourself at such a deep level and believe you can accomplish this?

To be completely honest, until I really dug deep down and examined my own core beliefs further, I couldn't win a tennis championship. Sure, I earned a world-ranking on the professional tour and traveled the globe playing at a very, very high level of tennis—but I didn't *win* championships. And yes, I had moments of brilliance, and took down some really great players from time to time—but at the core, my belief system did not believe I could actually win the tournaments.

Because, without thoroughly believing that I *could* win, my final outcome was already written. So, without further delay, let's pair up this principle #1 with the animal that's going to anchor that very powerful concept.

What becomes habit

We use the armadillo—actually two armadillos in this step. The reason we have two, is that the conscious mind and the subconscious mind are two parts of our brain that work together. But, it's the conscious mind that is the gateway to the subconscious mind. And it is in the subconscious realm is where all our habits lie.

To illustrate, let's do a little exercise. Whether you are sitting or standing, it doesn't matter. Simply fold your arms—one over the other however it comes naturally for you. Now let me ask you a question. Did you have to think about doing that?

Probably not. It just happened automatically. Well, that came from the subconscious mind. After we have received imprint after imprint into the subconscious mind, it becomes a habit—and we subliminally operate our lives. Sometimes it is in "hoodwink" or negative conditioning, and sometimes it's in total control and when we are aware of it.

53

Now what I'd like you to do is drop your arms down by their sides, and then fold them one more time. This time, take a look at which arm is on top. It will either be the left or right. If you've got any more than that, well... let's go into business together and I might be able to make some money off of you by selling you some swamp land in Florida!

All kidding aside, what I'd like you to do now is to again drop your arms down to your sides, and then fold them for a third time, but this time do it exactly opposite from the time before. If you were right over left, then swap to left over right, and vise versa. How did that go for you? Was it somewhat awkward? You may even have had to try one or two times before getting it right—that is not all that unusual, really.

Why did this feel awkward or uncomfortable? Well, it wasn't your body, I can assure you of that. It was the subconscious mind recognizing that you've changed up something. It made you feel a little uncomfortable at first. And, if we're not careful, as Roger would say, if we are "wussies," what we'll do is retreat and go back to what felt comfortable to us.

This is so important. And, I keep it in mind when I am teaching and training my clients. I always take them just a little bit beyond their comfort zones. They feel a little awkward at first, but through persistence and determination, it eventually becomes a habit. Then, it doesn't matter which way we fold our arms—the subconscious mind will now accept it. It is through these regular imprints that we make progress.

A simple shift in your beliefs

One time I worked with a talented young professional tennis player, named Vince Spadea, who at the time was ranked #357 in the ATP rankings. After just a short time working on his mental mindset, he quickly rose to #52 in the world rankings (then into the top 20) which was faster than anyone had done before—and all by simply shifting a belief he had about himself.

While we were working out on the court, he told me "I just don't have any weapons." His belief system was that he didn't have that big powerful thing that would enable him to win the crucial points.

54

So, when those big and crucial points came—and they inevitably did—he faltered. And when he was playing a top-ranked player, his belief system reinforced that he just didn't have the weapons needed to beat them.

Now, what do you think happened? He'd play a close game, but when the big points came up, he would step down instead of stepping up. However, while I was hitting with him and watching him play, I saw how early he picked up balls off the bounce. It was easy for me to see that this was a *huge* weapon, but he had never thought of it as that.

I simply pointed out to him, "Vince, your hands are so quick. They're the fastest hands I've ever seen! You pick up the ball so early. That's a powerful, powerful weapon!" He said, "Really? They are?" He literally was in disbelief. He had been so concerned with looking for some "secret weapon," that he clearly missed what was already within his own talents.

Then, I told him that, in fact, what he did was exactly what Andre Agassi (who at the time was the #1 player in the world) did—but even better! Agassi was known for his quick return of serves and for picking up the ball early. Vince certainly had a tremendous weapon.

Although it surprised him to hear this, he changed his perspective and began to adopt this as truth. And, with this new belief, he took on pressure points with a confidence like never before. Instead of focusing on his weakness, he began to step into his strengths. I've never had a client change his beliefs so quickly before. But, I could see it in his eyes; Vince believed this as soon as it was spoken.

Finding your core strengths

Usually it takes some work and some time to integrate a stronger belief in oneself, but Vince went on to win the very next tournament, beating two players in the top 75 in the world. Before that, he had not beaten anyone in the top 100, but he got to the semi's and then lost in 3-sets. He could have gotten into the finals, but his belief system wasn't quite ready for that. And yet, he had been able to advance at least that much because he now knew he had a weapon.

Think about this. It's all about how you look at things. And in crucial situations, when you have a solid belief system that supports you to get through it, that's completely different from a belief system that says, "Oh no, I can't do that!" Obstacles will stay there and block your path. But young Vince was able to shift his perspective and knew he did in fact have a weapon.

And, what is really cool about this is Vince went on to beat Agassi both times he had to face him that year. Which incidentally, were two of Agassi's only four losses during that period of time—that's just amazing!

Seeing unseen opportunities

The same goes for business. Recently, I was working with the CEO of a large architectural and real estate development company, and as we talked I discovered one of his own limiting beliefs. He told me about how every time there was a "downturn in the economy" his firm would struggle—and to a logical mind that makes perfect sense. Why would he think anything different?

However, to a creative mind—and one that doesn't live "in the conditions" but goes around them—unseen opportunities begin to magically appear. After digging into this, and showing him just how easy it is to shift those limiting beliefs into more life-giving ones, his whole outlook changed. No longer is he "buying into the struggle" and his new beliefs are becoming the new normal for him. He is seeing more and more opportunities and grabbing on to them.

Again, this is because we *shifted* his beliefs about him working in an "up and down" business environment that was prone to cycles. Now, when things appear to be crashing down all around him—and when he would previously be sucked into the energy of struggle—he looks for the opportunities that might be just under the surface. By shifting these thought patterns of default, he began to take on what previously appeared to be obstacles, and turned them to opportunities.

Elevate your belief system

Did you know that there were more millionaires made in the "Great Depression" than ever before? I'm not saying those weren't challenging times, and that a lot of people didn't struggle. It just means that there is always more to life and business than meets the eye.

56

The power of your belief system can take you down into struggle—or it can elevate you to your highest good. What is needed is an understanding of just how powerful your thoughts are, and knowing that truly, "It is done to you as you believe."

In tennis, I became #1 in the senior divisions later on by "training my mind" to believe it was possible. By doing this, my work habits became better, and fed this newfound confidence and belief.

With more empowering beliefs and these new mental triggers at my side—and in this case the animal trigger is two armadillos—every time I began to get sucked back into my old limiting belief system, I used this anchor system to propel me through. For me, this is what living in "Beast Mode" truly means.

What are some beliefs you might need to support a high level of focus during competition or in business?

Focus on what you love and reinforce that daily. If you woke up every morning and started the day with positive affirmations, and ended your day each night with those same affirmations, your subconscious mind would then begin to believe it was possible to receive all of that which you desire. When you see your results in advance and in your mind achieving those things you desire, your belief system grows and grows, and is able to allow it in or to bring it into existence.

Doing consistent mental practices builds your belief system to support your desires. That which you feed grows, and that which you starve will die. Consciously choose the thoughts you want to feed. But, without consistency, it's easy to fall prey to those negative voices that will distract you from achieving your goals. Your "bigger you" naturally shows up once you take the time to tap into that inner strength through regular practice. Then, in time, your core beliefs will support a high level of focus on a regular basis.

To tint or taint – the choice is yours

Following ancient wisdom, "It is done unto you as you believe" and that goes all the way down to the core beliefs that are running your operating system—which is another way of describing your subconscious mind.

And, since your mind is a pretty powerful engine, make sure to feed it with positive and life-giving fuel. This will produce a protective barrier against negative influences and conditions. Don't allow "hoodwink" or negative influences to taint "who you really are."

As Roger would often say, "Habitually *tint* your mind with positive influences to form a protective barrier against the *tainting* effect of negative influences. When you do, you will achieve life mastery through this sort of mind mastery."

EXERCISE: List 5 negative beliefs you could release that no longer serve you?

For example: 1) A huge negative belief to release might be any thoughts of "well these are the cards I was dealt." Become the dealer and play the cards you want to play. 2) Negative words lead to negative action. Be aware of the words you speak, for they truly lead the way to your thoughts that create your actions. 3) You are all alone and don't have the power to tap into a force stronger and wiser than you. Einstein didn't have a bigger brain: he simply took the time to connect to that source that is available to all. 4) Don't let others tell you what your reality is because it will be tainted with their own limiting beliefs. 5) Know who you truly are, made in the image of your maker, with the same power to create. You have been given "free will," so freely choose your life and practice daily stepping into a life that you truly love.

When I think about myself in all the things that I have done, if I didn't have a system to support my beliefs, I would fall short. My subconscious mind ruled the day—and it didn't necessarily believe I could do it. So, your belief system truly shapes everything you do.

Therefore, you are going to want to feed your mind constantly—especially your subconscious mind—with positive reinforcement of what you want to achieve. This is so your mind starts to *believe* in it. You want your inner mind in harmony with your outer mind. That's why I love the principle of MIMA & LIMA.

58

Mind Mastery = Life Mastery

Animal Instinct Principle: MIMA & LIMA

"Habitually tint your mind with positive influences to form a protective barrier against the tainting effect of negative influences. When you do, you will achieve life mastery through this sort of mind mastery."

– Roger Anthony

And so again, the armadillos are great examples of fortifying our beliefs and the foundations from which our lives are built upon. Why? Well, for one, because they have armor. That's why they're called armadillos.

This armor is protection from outside threats—and if they are indeed threatened, they just roll up into a ball. In that way, they're completely protected and anything that's an outside threat just bounces off of them.

What types of negative threats do we face as human beings? Negative conditioning or negative concerns are a couple of them. Worry, doubt, and fear are some more. So if we act like the armadillo, and put up our armor as a shield of protection from all of the negative influences that bombard us and threaten the health and well-being of our minds, we can simply let all of that bounce off without having any negative imprints.

Putting on the protective armor

We can do this with the conscious mind to prevent any negative influences from ever entering into the subconscious mind by putting up our protective armor there too. This way we can take control of our lives by making sure we imprint nothing but positive.

The names of our armadillos are MIMA and LIMA, which simply stands for "MI-nd MA-stery" and "LI-fe MA-stery." Simply put—Mind Mastery equates to Life Mastery. Which is key in terms of the negative things and conditioning we face in life.

Another way of looking at this is—mastering our lives and learning from the failures. Which world do you want to live in? It's all about controlling the mind and only allowing that which is supportive to that which we want to achieve or receive.

It's all about getting to that focus of *believing* that you can accomplish whatever you desire—no matter what.

The key that unlocks unlimited potential

This is important. Everything I teach and everything Roger taught are all about the ways we think. Our minds hold a key that unlocks our potential. It has nothing to do with the body. Sure you've got to have physically strong bodies. You've got to keep them fit especially as professional athletes but the big key is how much of it is mental attitude? How much of it is extreme focus? Once you get the hang of this and are able to choose your thoughts and up-level your core beliefs, amazing things just start coming "out of the blue." You'll begin to have "game changing" moments in every area of your life and more and more often.

One of my son's, Shane, who is a starting quarterback in the AFL indoor arena professional football league, says it so well. He says, "It's when preparation and dedication meet opportunity." You see he is a perfect example of someone who is willing to do the prep and whatever it takes to be at the top of his game. And by prep, I'm talking about the "mental prep" just as much as physical prep, training, and conditioning. It's the full package. That is how champions are born.

You may have heard me say, "I don't care what you do in life, it doesn't matter what you do, these principles work." Well, that's true. And, they work in every area of your life, not just sports, not just in business, but in *every* aspect. But, it takes a set of deep core beliefs.

So, how do you build a belief system that goes all the way down to your core to support this? It's your prep. It's your visualizations, it's setting your intentions, and then following through on your intentions. It is your affirmations, it is your acknowledgments of the wins you have each and every day. That is what it truly takes to rebuild your beliefs. It takes consistency and practice, and it also takes discipline.

And so, armadillos strangely enough can choose to blow themselves up with air and literally float across the water to get away from their enemies. Or they can exhale all that air and literally sink to the bottom and crawl along the sand.

60

But, you and I know that the best way of doing it is to rise above it all and float right across the top of the water. Don't sink to the bottom. Don't let the negatives take a hold of you and weigh you down.

As noted before, during our journey of transformation, we will undoubtedly discover more about "who we really are" and "what we are truly capable of." And, it really is all about discovery—discovery of self, the real me, and the real you. We're not looking for the hoodwinked, closed, unaware and restricted self, but the open, willing, aware and unrestricted self that lies within each of us—the true spirit of who we really are.

The journey towards our higher self cannot start until we have moved out of the territory of closed (unwilling) and unaware, and into the territory of open (willing) and aware. The tricky part is that we have all been hoodwinked into being closed to some degree. We've got to learn to be more open.

Do you consider it an advantage or a disadvantage to have strong beliefs?

Remember this is up to you. A strong belief that your conditions rule your life is a disadvantage. A strong belief in being a creator of your life is a major advantage. So, knowing how important your beliefs are, support your beliefs through preparation and daily practice.

I believe in you. Do you believe in you? When MLB Luke Scott's mom asked him when he was only eight, what do you want to be when you grow up? He told her "I want to be big league baseball player." She simply replied, "Well, someone has to, why not you?" He went on to have a successful major league career.

So then, what do you want to be? No matter what age you are, choose what you truly love and let your desire fuel your power to achieve. When I met Peg South, she was 85 years old and was the "65 and over" national champion in tennis. And, she didn't take up the game until she was 69. She inspired me to know my age didn't matter. It was my belief system that did!

The more open and willing we are, the more aware we become. The overriding influence that enables us to move from closed unawareness to open awareness is SAPA (Self-Awareness and Positive Attitude). Open awareness unveils our degree of SAPA, which is basically how we feel about ourselves.

Our degree of SAPA is directly connected to our level of Self-Mastery—and by now you've figured out that true success is also the product of Self-Mastery. Self-Mastery and success will become easier as you make them habitual. In fact, true success is moving from "conscious awareness" to subconscious habit.

Self-defeating behaviors lead to failure

Unfortunately, a great percentage of hoodwinked people in the educated world never achieve true success, because they never move out of closed unawareness. Their state of closed unawareness is a cycle of self-defeating behavior that can only lead them to failure. The result of closed unawareness is inevitably low SAPA, less success, and lack of Self-Mastery. And because unawareness is a choice, we are really only defeated by ourselves.

On the other hand, positive cycles of Self-Mastery can only encourage self-victorious behaviors that lead to high SAPA. Thus we achieve victory over self—and thereby ensure that we are leading and taking charge of our own destinies. That is a powerful place to be.

EXERCISE: List 5 positive beliefs you would like to add that will support your future goals?

Take the time right now, grab a pen and pad. Quietly open to your mind, and write these 5 beliefs you would like, that could take you to new heights. Be open to ideas that will help you grow these beliefs.

Just by getting into the energy of your desires, you will be lifted into a state of frequency to achieve. Just like tuning into your favorite radio or TV station. No problem is solved in the energy of the problem. Every answer and solution lies in a higher frequency. So, allow yourself to soar and come *from* your desires, rather than trying to *get* to them.

The armadillos, MIMA & LIMA, have this armor around them, which is a great visual cue that says we need to protect our mind from being bombarded with negative thoughts and influences. Once again, the principle of Mind-Mastery equals Life-Mastery, which means we need to habitually tint our mind with that which is positive to form a protective barrier against all the negative influences out there. Because every day we have lots of opportunities to have negative influences—it's a part of life.

You just need to back away a little bit and understand that the subconscious mind has no emotion and does not know fact from fantasy. It simply acts upon the information it receives. Then it steers us towards goals or targets, or in some cases away from our targets.

I was talking with one of my clients, and she recently became the "salesperson of the year." What an amazing feat, she had the #1 sales last year within the entire company. And, last week she had a great week of sales to kick off this year and stay right on track. But, she said to me, "I'm just so overwhelmed." To that I said, "Just stop!" Words are really powerful, and even if you want this business, but you keep saying you are overwhelmed, you will get more and more cause to being overwhelmed.

Don't give into that, because your subconscious is listening and it doesn't know if that is fact or fiction. And, you might not even hear on a conscious level what you just said, but your subconscious level is hearing it. So, what's going to happen is you are going to get overwhelmed with a lot of sales and this will prevent you from achieving more sales—because you have a belief system that makes you overwhelmed. Sometimes it's just shifting your whole approach. And, that can be just a slight shift.

Subconscious programming

Before we move onto Step Two, it is important to note that the subconscious mind does not have any emotion attached to it, and again, it can't tell fact from fiction. A key point to consider is that consciousness is the gateway to the subconscious—and this has everything to do with both our successes and our failures. It also increases our level of SAPA.

So keep in mind, the subconscious:

* Has no emotions
* Can't tell fact from fantasy
* Acts on information it receives
* Steers us toward given goals and targets

By utilizing both our conscious and our subconscious minds, and protecting ourselves from the negative influences that bombard us each and every day, we can increase the likelihood of achieving both personal and business success.

Achieve Life Mastery: Through Mind Mastery

It's time to form a protective barrier against the tainting effect of negative influences...

Implementation Checklist +Results:

* Harmony In – Harmony Out
  or
* Hoodwink In – Hoodwink Out
* Constructive Self-Talk and Thoughts = Constructive Actions
* Destructive Self-Talk and Thoughts = Destructive Actions

What are the results of this? When we reprogram and replace tainted thought patterns (negative) with tinted ones (positive), we change our thought paradigms.

Chapter 2

NOBO™ (The Flying Fish)

In This Chapter

* Finding potential where others only see limitations
* Learning to move away from obstacles and roadblocks
* Discarding the principle of "out of the box" thinking

"During my career, I've worked with Dave and without him – let's just say I definitely prefer working with him."

– Scott Feldman, pitcher, Texas Rangers

As we continue learning about the "12-Step BE A BEAST Process," we go right from taking a look at our beliefs and how that guides and shapes our lives, right into examining "perceived limitations" and potentialities. I like how well these two steps tie-in together. The bottom line is, if we focus on our weaknesses, our own unique gifts aren't able to shine. So, why does this occur?

It's because, our attention is mainly being directed on "what we *don't* have" rather than what we do. This is a common thing most of us face, since there is plenty of people out there who are only too quick to point out our weaknesses—especially in sports.

You see, in sports there is a scoreboard. And, there are all sorts of analysts and reporters whose jobs are to point out the teams, players, or opponents weaknesses. The problem is most players can't get that stuff out of their head. Sure, there are those who use this to fuel their performance by "showing them" they are wrong. But, for many professional and amateur athletes, this only gets their focus off-track and gets in their head.

Let me point out that this is *not* about avoiding our weaknesses. It's more about focusing on what our strengths are, and being aware of what you know and what you don't know. If you aren't a technical kind of person, and you need to have that kind of problem solved, hire someone who knows what they are doing to help you out. Don't try to be good at everything or try to please everyone. Stay in your area of genius, then delegate those areas you're not as strong in.

Find Potential vs. Limitations

You'll hear me often say, "There's always a potential lying right beside any perceived limitations" and those that only *appear* to be blocking your path. In this chapter, we'll look at what's limiting these potentials in any area of your life—then assist you in moving past them. We will also explore methods to "change the channel" and assist with tapping into the unlimited potential that lies before us.

In reference to the point I was making about just how "technologically challenged" I am, and how my kids always give me a hard time for this—let me just say this they think it is pretty funny and get a good laugh over it. But, I have two choices here. I can get down on myself and struggle with whatever it is, and believe I'm downright dumb for not being able to "get" this techie stuff (and I'm talking pretty low tech stuff like how to use the features on my iPhone!) and bring that energy into everything else I do. Or, I can focus on the things I do really, really well—like being a coach.

It's not hard to imagine, but I love to coach—and I'm a damn good one at that. I really love inspiring people and taking them higher and to new ground—whether it's in sports or business. And, that's what I focus on.

Then, I allow capable people—who are way better at all of those other things—to support me in that. This is what I call a "win-win" and a perfect model of cooperation, community, and collaboration—which is vital in moving us forward in life.

Shine a flashlight on those limitations

I had a baseball client who played for the Cincinnati Reds tell me one of his limitations was that he didn't have great mobility or fast enough lateral movement, and as a shortstop it was keeping him from advancing to the next level. I told him to keep working physically toward better lateral movement, but what truly changed this limitation into great lateral movement is when I changed his "mental" focus. I helped him to see the ball earlier and to be more aware of the pitch, it's location, and then to zero in on the swing of the batter.

What happened then was, he began to see *where* the ball was going sooner, so he was in turn able to get to those balls he had never before been able to reach. His range and lateral movement improved dramatically. As a result he ended moving up from Double A to Triple A and then into the major leagues.

When we flip a "perceived limitation" on its side, and turn it into an advantage, magic happens. This player didn't hide from the limitation, we just put a flashlight on it and found the positive that was lying right beside it—and used that to create a positive outcome and potential rather than staying within the limitation.

Moving Past Obstacles

Focus On The Possibilities

"If you can dream it, you can do it."

– Walt Disney

My grandfather, who at the time was the executive vice-president of Bell Telephone, had an entrepreneur come to him who was millions of dollars in debt. This man's brother accompanied him—an accountant who was worried and only saw the investors debit columns.

But, this young entrepreneur who was living inside the potential of his dream was more like, "Oh my, you mean that many people believe in us?" This only excited him more and with this enthusiasm, he came to my grandfather for additional support.

This young man came to my grandfather with a crazy concept of a "theme park" with all these different make-believe lands and a mouse—it was quite a wild dream. My grandfather liked the idea and said yes—he agreed to jump in with financial support. And, with this first big "yes" from the largest telephone company in the world at the time, things began to take off—and more and more companies also said yes.

Often, it only takes one "yes" to get things rolling. And, that is how things happen—by focusing on the possibilities and not the limitations. That is precisely what Walt Disney did way back then, and the rest, as they say, is history! He kept the possibilities in his mind and pictured how magical it all could be. Unlike his brother, whose sole focus was clearly on the debt. Of course, part of growing a business is the likelihood you could go into debt. Even so, stay *in* the vision.

As a young kid, I never could understand why this guy named Disney would send *us* a big 'ol box of presents every Christmas, and on each gift card he'd say, "Thank you" to us! What? Give us presents and also be the one saying thank you? It was pretty crazy—but crazy good!

Imagined or perceived weaknesses

So, here we are at Step Two, which is where we find potential—when others might only see the limitations. It's where we take a look at what is limiting ourselves and our potential in all areas of our lives, and where we assist you in moving past these obstacles—since they are really only *perceived* limitations anyway.

I have a personal belief, that lying right next to any limitation is an equal or even greater potential. It's just where you want to put your focus and which direction you face. If you make a decision to shift all your attention into the possibilities, you are then lifted into your strengths—and not lost in your weaknesses that only disguise and hide your strengths.

Even so, it's essential to acknowledge that we all have weaknesses, but, when we look at them instead as a potential strength—meaning turning those weaknesses into strengths—it makes a phenomenal difference. We can then accept weaknesses, because they lead us to our higher purpose. And then, we become stronger as a result of understanding that none of us is perfect.

Our animal instinct to anchor this is a flying fish of all things. Now, think about this for a moment in regard to our strengths. A flying fish was designed, like all fish, to breath in water. And yet, I've seen flying fish when they are being chased by an enemy literally launch out of the water, and not just go straight back in, but fly up to a quarter of a mile in distance—in an environment they weren't meant to breath in!

The name we have for this flying fish is NOBO, which stands for "NO BOundaries, NO BOx." And so, when we acknowledge that there really is no limit to human endeavors—then there really are no limits at all. Just think what would have happened if Walt Disney had succumbed to the "limited thinking" of his accountant brother? What Walt did was NOBO thinking. He stayed *out* of the box, because in fact, he had no concept that there even was a box.

Are you thinking "outside" the box?

So, every time you start doubting, and feel like you are slipping back into a box—stop and say "NOBO." That one word triggers a new type of thinking that reminds you of what Roger was known for saying, "Why am I even thinking about being *outside* the box? There *is* no freaking box, mate!" Simply stated, by claiming there is a box, means you *believe* there is a box. Shift into NOBO thinking and you will be without boundaries.

All of the great things in life, have been done by those who were crazy enough to believe they could be done. They did not live in a box—not a one of them. Like Steve Jobs once said, "Those who are crazy enough to think they can change the world, are the ones who do."

That's just how it is. There's never been an Olympics where there has not been a record broken. And, in my opinion, there never will be. We just get better, and better, and better. When we look at NOBO (as it relates to professional athletes and those that are up

69

and coming pros), we see in the field of life just how important it is to remember, "No boundaries, no freaking box!"

There are many times when you hear people saying, "Think outside the box," but really what we've done here is to "blow up the box." There is no box. There is no limit to what you can do. This is absolute. The minute we say, "Think outside the box," what does that represent? That there *is* a freaking box. So, what we'd like to do here is stress the importance of being like NOBO the flying fish—NO BOundaries, NO BOx.

Can you just see it now? You're on the playing field, whether that is in sports or in the work place, and you're in a NOBO way of thinking. That means, "I can do anything. I'm not limiting myself to anything." As opposed to people getting constricted and all bogged down with questions such as, "Can I do this?" or "How do I do this?" Rather than go down that path, simply blow up the box and as Nike says, "Just do it."

EXERCISE: List 5 limitations you believe are standing in the way of your intended success?

Remember the story of the baseball player who shifted his lateral movement through mental awareness? Don't be afraid to allow the perceived limitations out into the light of day. Otherwise, when you stuff them down inside, they are always still there and bound to sneak up on you when you least expect them. Instead, it's better to let them out in the open and once they are, you can then move on and into your true strengths. So, take a minute now to list 5 things that you believe may be standing in the way of your success.

In the last chapter, I talked about how after turning his perceived limitations into a strength, Vince Spadea essentially became the ATP Tour's "fastest rising star" and climbed the world-rankings from #357 to #52 in just six months (and shortly after rose into the 20's).

Mistakenly, Vince thought he "had no weapons" and saw that as his biggest limitation. This is precisely why he had not broken into the top 50. It simply took someone from the outside looking in to give Vince a glimpse of the weapons he already possessed.

This rapid rise in the world rankings also meant his income rose from about $20-30,000 in winnings up into the millions. That's the kind of impact a mental shift in your thinking can have on your bottom line. Keeping this in mind, what big weapon or unique quality in you might be hidden or overlooked?

Which limitations can you shift into a positive potential?

In professional sports, you have scouts out there analyzing every little thing about the players. One of my ballplayers I worked with was an all-star in Triple A—he hadn't been able to get up into the majors yet and was fighting tooth and nail to get up there. One day he came into the locker room before the game and saw this book that had the scouts notes on every player in baseball.

So, he went to his name to see what they were saying about him, and it was based on a five-star system. He saw that for power he had 4 stars, and since he was leading the league in home runs that was to be expected, even though he thought he should have been rated a 5. Then he saw arm strength, and it was a 1-star. Next was for speed, and again it was a 1-star. He was an outfielder, and on defense he had been given a 1-star also.

Now he could have been crushed at that moment and just thrown in the towel because this was basically saying he'd never get in the major leagues, because that is just how they look at that sort of thing. But instead, he used it as fuel and got inspired once we talked about this. As it turned out, a player in the majors got hurt and my client got pulled up for a two-week window to fill in. Well, he never looked back and once he got this chance to play for the Houston Astros, he ended up leading the team in every category and became the hottest hitter in all of baseball for the second half of that season.

As in the case of the Houston Astros player, whoever gave him a 1-star for speed sure looked pretty stupid when he proceeded to beat out balls that he hit to the shortstop—that's very hard to do and you have to be really quick to do it. And that was this players proudest moment—whoever gave him a 1-star speed had only motivated him more. The same with this players rating for defense in the outfield—he went on to almost never making any errors. I think it was something like 98%, which is a pretty amazing stat.

So, where do these things come from? When it comes to limitations, either we will put them on ourselves, or we will let others put them on us. Never put yourself into a box. That's why I love the anchor here, NOBO.

I once worked with a volleyball player who thought she was too small to play for a Division 1 college. At least that is what she had been told, and therefore had adopted that belief about herself. I shifted her focus towards how much more athletic and quick she was because of the fact that she was not so tall and lanky.

This client was able to shift her focus and rapidly improved her chances of getting a scholarship to a great program. In fact, she ended up not getting just one Division 1 offer, but several great D1 scholarship offers—just by having a simple shift in perception and turning what looked like a limitation into a strength and potential.

"Out Of The Box" Thinking

Animal Instinct Principle: NOBO

"Throw ALL of the fish from your nets up and onto the boat for sorting. Then if one of them is not something you want to keep, simply throw it overboard and off the boat, leaving only those you want as keepers"

– Dave Austin

Too often we stop short and don't tap into our true gifts and creativity—because of judgments. Many of the thoughts that run through our head are, "Is this idea good or bad? Stupid or brilliant?" Who knows until we gather all of these ideas up and bring them to the surface? Who cares if every idea isn't a keeper? Who cares if it may sound stupid or dumb?

It comes right back to our judgments. And in this process, not only do we judge ourselves, but we also judge others and hold them back from their own greatness as well. When I was co-writing *Songwriting for Dummies* with Grammy Award-winning and platinum album-selling songwriter, Jim Peterik, he told me a great story about the time when he was asked to co-write a song with Sammy Hagar.

72

Both Jim and Sammy were very successful in their own rights, and both had written big hit songs—think "Eye of The Tiger" for one—so they were excited to be co-writing together.

After about a half hour into their writing session, nothing had been put to paper. Finally, after noticing the block that was obviously happening, Sammy said, "I guess I'm just afraid of saying something dumb." And, Jim agreed, saying it was the same for him.

As crazy as it may sound, each had such great respect for the other's talents, that individually they were feeling the pressure and afraid of not coming up with something brilliant—in order to perhaps impress the other and validate themselves in the process.

Luckily for them, they agreed that it was okay to come up with some "dumb ideas" in order to get started. Then, once the pressure was off, they eventually wrote one of Sammy's all-time biggest hits—and all within a half hour worth of non-judgmental effort.

You see, we worry so much about "what others will think," that we actually block the great ideas just waiting to be let out. Like I said, crazy as it sounds, we all do this to some extent. But don't. Because, being concerned about what "others" will think about you is mainly a wasted and unnecessary thing to do.

Step into a NOBO land way of thinking

Something similar occurred when I was working on the "mental mindset" with a client who is an architect. We dove into this very same concept, and by allowing whatever ideas came into his head to be considered whether they seemed good or bad, he eventually won the bid competition for a large project. Afterwards, he told me he simply went into "NOBO land," which allowed for those brilliant solutions to just show up.

As mentioned before, you never want to hide from your perceived weaknesses. A better idea is to shine a light on them, so they can no longer sneak up and keep you from seeing the real strengths you already have.

Keep feeding your strengths—since what you starve will die, and what you feed will grow.

With the pro athletes I coach, there are always those around them who point out what they see as the players' weaknesses. This is common, and often times these people *mean well* and *believe* they are only helping. But, as I said above, what you focus on expands. Instead, and what I am suggesting, is to be sure to spend more time focusing on your strengths.

Of course, you can acknowledge your weaknesses and perceived limitations, but only in an effort to learn and grow to improve your skills. I will point out once again, if you turn your attention to finding the strength that lies right next to any of these "perceived" weakness, they will be transformed into strengths, and you will end up being able to perform great feats.

Too small to compete

I have a client who, as a quarterback in football, was constantly being told he was too small to play at the next level. This began in youth football and continued all the way into the pros. He could have easily bought into these "limiting beliefs" and allowed that to keep him from his dream to play professionally.

But, he didn't. Instead of being stuck or labeled in that perceived limitation, he rose above it and focused on his unique strengths. He worked on his skills and footwork, and developed "quick feet," which many of the taller quarterbacks did not have. He also worked on perfecting a quick release and tight spiral throws.

In turn, this quarterback not only went on to break almost every passing record at his high school, but then went on, and against all odds, to earn a full-ride scholarship to play D1 college football. And now, as a professional player, he continues to set records.

The key is to look at the potentials that are lying right beside what most would consider limitations. I could easily write another dozen or so stories of the great successes I have witnessed personally from living just this principle—simply because it really is that important and that effective.

Make it a new winning habit to stay grounded in your gifts and not all of those negative things that bug you.

The NOBO thinking mindset

Take a look at great NFL quarterbacks such as Russell Wilson and Drew Brees. What a shame it would have been if either Russell or Drew had bought into the belief that being 6 feet tall or less, made it impossible to play professional football. Incidentally, my client is similar in size and talent to these Superbowl winning QBs. Neither of these two NFL greats, nor my client, bought into that way of thinking—neither should you.

Be sure to remember there is a positive or a polar opposite solution to every perceived weakness. And, you will always find these answers by living within this NOBO thinking mindset. Don't let the opinions of others encourage you into having "self-limiters" about your own performances—whether they be in sports, in business, or in any other area of your life.

So many times I have come across athletes, whether it's in youth sports, middle school and high school, or even at the college level and beyond, who are coached by those, who incidentally has never actually played in the pros, only to have their coaches' own limiting beliefs projected onto them. This is a real shame—and please don't ever let this happen to you.

What I hear all the time and what these young athletes are being told is, "Well don't even think about it. Do you know *how good* you have to be to play in the pros? You really don't have what it takes." Again, these are just limiting beliefs and not even your own. Please don't let this happen to you—you have enough other things to think about. When I have a client who is being told these sorts of things, we immediately go to work to remove these "limitations" to reprogram them into more positive strength building beliefs and thought patterns—and not just those that were put inside their heads by someone else.

Three "thoughts" from gold

In Napoleon Hill's life-changing book "Think and Grow Rich," he tells the story of R.U. Darby and his uncle and how they were caught up in the "gold fever" during the great California Gold Rush. They came out from Maryland to stake their claim. They worked with just a pick, and after a few weeks they were rewarded with finding gold. They went back home and raised money to buy machinery so they could dig deeper.

These newly made miners found more gold and their excitement grew. But then, as they continued to dig deeper and deeper they found no more gold and ran out of money. They thought they had come to the end of their rainbow, and finally decided to give up.

They sold their machinery and mine to a junk man for pennies on the dollar. The junk man, also knowing nothing about mining, called in an expert engineer to help, and with his advice, dug three feet to the left of where the original two minors gave up. This small adjustment is what eventually led them to finding millions of dollars worth of gold, simply because the junk man knew enough to seek out expert advice.

A few years ago, Sharon Lechter and Greg Reid wrote a great book called, "Three Feet from Gold: Turn Your Obstacles into Opportunities" to fully illustrate this point. How many times has something like this happened to you? I know for me it has happened all too many times. That's precisely why I now surround myself with mentors and coaches who help me to see what is lying right outside my own picture frame.

EXERCISE: List 5 positive potentials for each limitation.

Take a look at your list of 5 limitations, and beside each one of these write out as many potential strengths you might uncover that will transform these limitations into positives. Have fun with this. Don't let judgments or the "how" stop you from writing down great possibilities and outcomes. And think about this, just by simply listing these potentials, you are that much closer to living them. With this new level of focus, your eyes will begin to see things you had never seen before. But don't be too hard on yourself—it's only because without knowing it your worries and concerns were keeping you from seeing with clearer vision.

Again, I am a big believer that right next to any limitation lies an equal or greater potential. So, where is your own personal gold mine? It is between your ears? And, learning to "get your mind to work for you rather than against you" simply takes daily practice. This is where real opportunity truly meets preparation. When you begin to look at every "perceived" obstacle as an opportunity, you will surely realize that we are always just "three positive thoughts" from gold.

76

So, find out what your true gifts are, and then blossom those. That is a major key to life—when you begin to pay attention and notice more, everything changes.

Many times we just go through life day-to-day, and we don't really pay attention to what we are doing—we might not even be aware of what we are thinking. That is when we are hanging out in the world of limitations, and not in a life of possibilities.

So, how important is it to you?

Seriously, a flying fish? They weren't made to even breath in the air, let alone fly! And there are videos that have captured them being able to fly for two whole miles! Think about this for a minute. One, they don't have wings, and two, they can't breath out of the water. So, how do they do it? We can learn much from this kind of example. Now bring this back to your life situation. What differences in the outcomes do you believe will occur if you incorporate some of these mental shifts? I have learned from experience, when you *bull-shift* your mind, everything is possible—and I mean everything!

Remember what my architect client says, "I just need to go to NOBO land." And, when he goes to NOBO land, he is able to create the most amazing designs. With this type of thinking, there is no box to limit us in any way. We need to have no more of this, "Well, I'm thinking outside the box" mentality.

Simply blow up the box! The very fact that you think there is a box means your mind is limiting you and you are not advanced enough. Blow up that box—there is no box, and there are no boundaries!

This is ultimately true, but it takes a real trust. It takes feeding your belief system on a daily basis and in a way that supports you at a deeper level. It takes a deep trust to open yourself to being all that you can be, and know you can tap into a strength in you that is so far greater than you give yourself credit for. But, of course, you live with yourself. Who are you to be so great? Well, who are you not to be so great!

To further this point, in tennis, the great players watch the swing of their opponents' racquet—and know right away if they are hitting with under-spin or top-spin.

This helps them to get into position way before the ball even crosses the net towards their side. Beginners, however, wait for the ball to bounce before they determine what to do. This means they are constantly in a "reaction" mode rather than an "action" mode.

This makes a big, big difference. Just remember that simple solutions are always there—we just need to keep our eyes open to the possibilities, and get counsel from those who have actually been there before. We can then, positively move forward and focus our thoughts on the gold that is at hand—which may only be three feet to the left and fully within reach.

Before we move onto Step Three, it is important to remember that NOBO thinking really does mean that there is "No Box – No Boundaries!" It is for us to step boldly into this way of thinking because we must:

* Realize there simply is no box

* Remove limiting judgments

* Be open minded to new possibilities

* Develop proactive thinking and actions

When we do this, we will fully be living up to our true potential and expanding our horizons in order to live a life of purpose and one that we were meant to live.

Learn Lateral Thinking By Daring To Be Different

Sometimes it may be necessary to boldly stand by ideas that are "out of the box," which initially could be judged as ridiculous. Even though an original idea may not be adopted, it could spawn the most brilliant of all ideas and decisions.

So, go out and adopt a NOBO way of thinking—and live in a world that has "no box and no boundaries."

Implementation Checklist +Results:

* Use as a benchmark to think outside the norm
* Dare to be different
* Think laterally

What are the results of this? We expand our comfort zone and develop new paradigms of thinking. Keep in mind that radical change requires radical thinking. By doing so, you open yourself up to realms of new possibilities and opportunities—which then develop into proactive thinking patterns and actions.

"It is through clarity of purpose
I am best able to move into
meaningful action, propelled by a
powerful desire to achieve."

Chapter 3

DEPUTIS™ (The Meerkat)

In This Chapter

* Turning dreams into goals with a timeline
* Planning for success by being well-organized
* Learning how to clarify your vision to get desired results

"Unleash your inner beast through the extreme focus and mental strength to compete at your highest level."

— Jeff Garcia, NFL All-Pro quarterback

One of my partners and I were recently given the opportunity to work with a high level task force at a Fortune 150 diversified financial services company. And, through our Beast Mode LIVE corporate training program and "mindset" tools, we were able to help them achieve greater performance driven results, in part through the system of DEPUTIS.

DEPUTIS is a system to clarify vision and direction. It's also a tool for project management and delegation, and a system of advanced goal-setting—for effective achievement toward goals through clarity of purpose.

My mom, bless her heart, who at 89 has been a long-time customer of this company for 75 years, asked me "How can you possibly make them any better? They are already the best!" But, one thing I have learned while working with high achievers, is there are always new heights to ascend to, navigate, and explore.

Dreams, Goals, And Timelines

Turn your dreams into goals with a timeline. What a concept! By using "Intentions" and "To Do Lists," we can structure a solid success plan for the next twelve months—and provide the tools to create a lasting and sustainable system of follow-through and organization.

In this chapter, we're going to offer simple and easy to implement structures and effective processes for you to organize your life on not only a daily basis, but also on a monthly and yearly basis as well. Once you set up a system and structured plan, success is but a very short distance away.

Sustainable Organization

Animal Instinct Principle: DEPUTIS

"You could never pay enough for the value our USA team received from Dave's style of 'mental performance' coaching. And, speaking from personal experience, this work is quite literally, priceless."

– Shiv Jagdav, head coach, USA Olympic field hockey

I have worked with 4 different MVP pro football and major league baseball players, and each of them set new, and even higher goals the very next year. Setting goals is the foundation for achieving that which you desire. Continued growth is exciting, as opposed to being complacent—which only leads to a very boring life. But, first you need to have a target to shoot for, in order to be able to hit that target.

Next up is Step Three, which is where we turn our dreams into "goals with the timeline."

Looking back on my personal experience of playing tennis at the professional level, initially I didn't set specific goals. And, guess what happened? I had mediocre results.

This is because I didn't have any specific targets to go after. I was basically just going from one tournament to another and playing my tennis matches—and hoping to win. But, once I finally learned how to set specific goals and could actually "see" these goals coming true (through my own unique visualization process), I then could move *into* my goals with greater consistency.

These specific targets became my driving force. And when I went out to practice, I had a laser-like focus, because I had a certain target I wanted to hit. I now had a specific goal. And yet, without having a target, how can any of us expect to hit the bull's-eye?

Systems and communities

The animal we have used to anchor this principle is the meerkat, and the reason for this is that they work so incredibly well within communities. The amazing thing about the meerkat is that they are so incredibly well organized. Just amazing creatures they are—as in everything they do is planned out carefully. They even have child minders. So, when they go out to forage for food, they leave the young with "minders" that look after them while the parents are away.

In the meerkat community, everything is set up and organized. They have a sentry to warn when there is danger. They have nursery pens. They know exactly where to hide when they need to. They make one tiny sound, one squeak, and they know exactly what it means. When the sentry makes that noise, the rest of the family scurries into the burrows without even thinking about it, because the system is so beautifully set-up and well-designed.

And so our animal trigger name for the meerkat is DEPUTIS, which relates to this beautiful system of goal-setting and organization. D-E stands for *describe,* as we want to clearly describe what it is you wish to achieve; and then the P-U stands for what is the main *purpose*? In other words, why do you want to do it?

83

This is important because the why increases the value. To help us understand, and to drive this value deeper into every fiber of our being, it's important that we visualize the future with having already achieved the goal. And, not to be thinking about "How am I going to achieve this," but to see it as though it's already done.

This is because the subconscious mind can't tell fact from fantasy. So, we lock it in and the mind becomes a goal-setting mechanism. By clearly *DEscribing* it, then we determine what is its' *PUrpose* is. Again, what is your why for achieving it? And then we put a *TImeline* to it, as in "when do we begin and when do we end?"

Eliminating the pressure points

How many times do we try to achieve a goal but we haven't put a timeline on it, and we then find ourselves invariably and over and over again scurrying around to finish it at the last moment? And, how well do we do something where we're under pressure trying to finish it at the last moment? This is why, with the principle of DEPUTIS, we always put a beginning time and an ending time to each goal.

So, the last bit to this animal instinct principle trigger is now that we've gotten you to *DEscribe* what is your *PUrpose* and your why, along with what is the *TImeline* in order to accomplish this task, we finish with what is your *Strategy*. At this point, we have you lay out the action steps and strategy necessary to do it.

This is precisely what I do with my athletes when I am giving them a "game ready" to get them "in the zone" and playing at the highest level possible. During this process, I get them out there on the field and tapping into the thrill of competition, but I also get their goals mentally fixed into their minds so they become a reality before the game has even begun.

In essence, the game is over before it has started. The results end up taking care of themselves naturally, because the mind is aligned with the goals in advance. The animal instinct principle of DEPUTIS helps us to remain calm and on task, simply because we have a well-thought out and complete plan for success.

Setting yourself up for success

You may or may not know this, but I've been blessed to have four amazing boys, and one of my sons has a brilliant example of goal-setting and the results you can achieve by doing so. This is my second son, and the one who played high school football, then college football, and is now playing professional football.

In high school, he set his season goals by writing them out on a piece of paper that he taped right next to his bedroom door—and every single day he looked at those goals. By doing this, he effectively set himself up for success by creating a system and a set of goals.

Creating a system helps your mind know that you are organized. It's also a way of organizing your thoughts. Every day, my son was able to see exactly. "This is where I'm headed today. This is where I'm going." Without a system such as this, he could have easily fallen trap to "just playing each game." Sort of like what I did with my tennis matches on the tennis tour.

Luckily for my son, he was able to develop a winning habit that supported his goals at an early age. At first, even he agreed that his goals were very aggressive and pretty much impossible to achieve. But he set his sights on what he wanted to do, and did not let himself be deterred. Even during week three, when he could see that he was far from being on track—he stayed the course. And, you know, when the season was finally over, he ended up achieving close to 98 percent of what he had posted on his doorway. Without that list, I believe he'd have been lucky to achieve even 50 percent of those goals.

See it as though it's already done

There is no doubt about it. The mind is a goal-seeking mechanism. So, be sure to set up in the mind what it is that you want to achieve, and then see it as though it's already done. Play the video in your mind over and over again, to solidify your goals and desires, and help your subconscious mind become familiar with that which it is currently unfamiliar with. See your goals as already being accomplished, and enjoy the process as you watch it all unfold within your actual experiences.

To set this point a little bit more, here is what Roger had to say about my son, Shane, who had written down some pretty lofty goals and proceeded to live them right into existence:

"Well, Shane is one of the most incredible young men that I've met, and the reason for that is he lives what you've taught him. I believe that a lot of who he is has happened because from a very early age you've been teaching him about the power of the mind. And one of the things I noticed about you, Dave, is that you're full of joy. That's why I love working with you and that's why I think we've been sort of anchored together and I'm glad that we are. But the great thing about Shane is that wherever he is, he's just composed. He's just a young man of great composure and nothing seems to faze him. Well, that comes from his subconscious mind being totally told what to do at all times through the DEPUTIS system that you've installed into his life."

You can't even imagine how much these words from Roger meant to my wife and me. As parents, we are very proud of the fine young men our boys have become, and to have it validated by someone we both admired and respected so much, it was an incredible moment for sure. And now, we want you to take that same system and install it into your own life—and it truly does work in every aspect of life.

For every area in your life

I was providing "mental performance" coaching to a D1 college football team, and a player came up to me in the locker room and asked in a whispered voice, "Hey coach, does this stuff work for school too?" I nearly had to hold back a quick laugh, and said, "Yes. That would be a BIG yes." You see, it is true that how you do anything is how you do everything—and these principles work. So, be sure to use these methods and mental mindset triggers in every aspect of your life.

For Roger, he started off applying them at a very young age in athletics, both in the rugby league and in cricket, and later on in soccer. But then when he turned 34, he went fulltime into teaching corporations. So again, it applies everywhere—whether that is in sports, business, or in life.

The key to achieving goals is to first know your goals, then state your goals and write them down, and most importantly, post your goals where you see them each day. So often we get motivated to write goals for the New Year, and then only three weeks later they are out of sight and out of mind. It is not a wonder that next December we can't understand why we weren't more successful in achieving our dreams and desires.

My family has an annual practice where we all get together at the beginning of the year to plan out our yearly goals and intentions. We have even created a template format where we can easily put it all down in writing and revise our goals every January.

Annual goals and vision statements

This is an important key to success—put them down in writing. Not just so you can post them and keep them somewhere to remind you of what your goals are, but the actual process of writing them down just seems to give them more life and added power. And then, each of us also asks the other family members to give their suggestions so we help keep each other accountable.

In general, what we have is a separate sheet for each of us, that includes the following format:

* Main "theme" for the year – your focus point
* 5 moderate goals – things you know you can do
* 5 stretch goals – things that will be harder to do
* A "Big Kahuna" goal – which is a goal you have no idea how to do it but would love it to happen.

Here's an example of what a *"Main Theme"* looks like, and what my wife, Cathy, chose for herself:

"To Step Into the Ease and Elegance of an Abundant Lifestyle Each and Every Day."

Next, we make a list of the top 5 things we are grateful for, since everything positive is amplified by gratitude. And, you can't ever have too much of that, right?

For example, here is a breakdown of one of our gratitude lists that covers each of the main areas in life, including health, relationships, wealth, business, and free time:

Gratitudes for 2015

* For the safety, excellent health and well-being that my family and I continue to enjoy.

* For the success and opportunities my family and I share together.

* For having $100,000+ bank balance at all times.

* For spending quality time with family, which includes regular get-togethers.

* For my new friends and business partners.

We also tie it all together with a *"Personal Statement"* which can look something like this:

"My focus for 2015 is to spend the majority of my work time devoted to writing and creative business pursuits that prove to be very financially profitable and satisfying, AND to complete all of my contracted writing projects AND to spend significant quality time with my family and friends, while enjoying the freedom to travel on great trips when I want, where I want, by whatever means I want, AND to continue to enjoy loving my life more and more each and every minute, day, and month."

The next thing we put down is an *"Intended 'State of Being' Statement,"* which for example could be:

"I will be Happy, Grateful, and Loving."

And then the last part of our annual goals sheet is the main *"Area of Improvement"* that we will each focus on for the entire year. For this one we ask each family member to make a suggestion, from their perspective, on what the others could improve on, and then we choose the one each would like to focus on, such as:

"To always respond and react in a kind, loving, and patient manner, and to really enjoy life."

Make sure when you are creating your annual goals and vision statement to be kind to yourself and others, and to help each other rise up into a newer and better person. It's tempting to point out all their flaws, but this is not the time to beat anyone up. This is the time to inspire and help each other rise up to achieve more.

So, let's see what you can come up with for your own goal-setting and vision statement. In addition to listing the 5 moderate goals, along with the other items that were discussed above, take a moment and get clear on what your top 5 goals will be for the next 12 months:

EXERCISE: List 4 stretch goals (the ones that are going to be somewhat of a challenge and where you will need to stretch a little outside your comfort zone in order to achieve them):

We will get into stepping outside of your comfort zones another time, but for now, just know that we want to do this sort of thing in smaller increments—rather than jumping off any cliffs right off the bat. Studies show that small, and incremental steps over time produce greater and longer lasting results. So, let's go ahead now and get started. Make a list of all your goals, then pick out the 4 that will best fit within the description we've set out for a "stretch goal."

A new "winning habit" to start is to get a notebook that will be your dedicated "goal-setting" journal. It is for you to write down all of this in one place. Begin at the first of each year, and as you go along, cross off what you have achieved and keep adding new ones to the list. Keep it as a perpetual goal-setting book, and after some time, you will really enjoy looking back to see just how much you were able to accomplish by being so focused and providing clarity to your goals.

EXERCISE: Now let's list your "Big Kahuna" (that's something you really want, but have no idea just how it might happen):

This is the fun one for me. Even so, there are some people who have a "there's no way possible I could do this..." attitude. If that sounds like you, then I'm going to ask that you set aside this notion for the moment. In this exercise, I want you to be free to dream and think about "what you would love." If money, or time, or connections, or knowledge, or resources were not an issue, what would you love to accomplish this year—what is your "Big Kahuna?"

If you really let yourself go, and allow all the fears, doubts, and worries to fall away while you do these goal-setting exercises, you will absolutely be amazed at what can happen—and you will get so much more out of this process than if you hold back and stay within what you think may be realistic or obtainable.

Recalibrate along the way...

The main thing about setting goals is that once you've done so, make sure it becomes a "new winning habit" by looking at them on a daily basis. It's so crucial to do this. A common trap, and the main criticism about setting goals is, here we are in January making our New Year's resolutions and we are all excited about them, but then by February or March, half of them have been forgotten or given up on! Here we are in late February saying something like, "Wait, what were my goals? I've already forgotten them!"

And when December rolls around and we go back to see what we've accomplished, and whether or not we hit our goals or missed them—it's too late to recover. It's way too late to wait until then to pull them out of the drawer. You need to be looking at your goals and recalibrating them along the way—and as mentioned, on a daily basis. That is how you turn goal-setting and resolutions into a magic formula. That is how you create success habits that support you.

Strengthen Your Vision

Plan For Success And Structure

> "In absence of clearly defined goals, we become strangely loyal to performing daily trivia, until we ultimately become enslaved by it."
>
> —Robert Heinlein

In my work as a mental performance coach, I ask my private clients to tell me "one thing" that is a very important goal for them. Once that is identified, I then support them each and every week to take action steps towards achieving that goal. It is truly amazing to see just how easy it can be to hit goals when you have a clear vision and support system in place.

I'm sure you've heard the expression, "Well that came out of the blue." The more clear you are with your desired outcomes, combined with taking continuous action steps towards those outcomes, then it just so happens that this "blue" starts showing up within your life—and on a regular basis.

In our "30-Day Beast Mode ON Challenge" group coaching sessions, we ask each participant to put their own *stake in the ground,* so to speak, and ask them to claim what they are going to achieve in a certain period of time. Then all of us, the challenge members and I, begin to support each other in whatever ways we can—and we start a friendly competition to see who will be the first ones to succeed. The race is on and everyone is going for the gold. It's a fun and creative way to support each other, and amazing results just seem to show up "out of the blue" for all.

Foundations of integrity

Roger Anthony has a great little book called, *Now I Understand,* and in that, there is a passage entitled, *"Foundations of Integrity: Eternal Values."* I'd like to share that with you here:

"All that I now seek to achieve is first measured against the foundation values of integrity and love upon which my life is structured. From these my standards flow and clearly govern the choices I make. NOW I UNDERSTAND, the standards in which we abide create the quality, harmony, and security of our lives. In the doing comes... Motivation toward Desired Outcomes through Values and Standards Congruent to Vision." – Roger M. Anthony

I love the above passage, and want to emphasize just how important it is to stay in integrity with everything you do. As Roger said, the foundations of integrity create the standards by which we live our lives. And by remaining in integrity at all times and building the foundation of our entire work and personal lives around this principle, we can achieve such greatness.

So, right now, let's build upon what we've learned so far, and what we are envisioning for our new and expanded self, to see where we need to go next.

There is a great animal principle that's not featured in the "12-Step BE A BEAST Process," but I still want to mention it because it makes a good point to consider. This principle is anchored by GOBAFO™ the monkey, and describes how sometimes we must "**go back** in order to move **forward**." For a brief moment, let's *go back* over the first principles we have covered so far, so that we can then again move forward.

The element of time

Now that we've moved from the principles of RESPA and NOBO—where we've learned how to relax, evaluate, strategize, have patience, and then move into action, as well as learned how to blow up the box in order to have unlimited thinking and potential—we continue in order to learn more through the principle of DEPUTIS, which is where we "plan through commitment." This is where we will examine some key elements that will contribute to our successful planning strategies.

The first of these elements is time. Now, time is one of the most valuable commodities we have—although we seem to be constantly battling to find more of it. Most often, we are making an effort to manage it more efficiently and effectively in order to have more control over our everyday lives. If you knew this already, then perhaps you also know that the greatest enemy of time is it's adversary—procrastination!

In this next section we'll seek a clear understanding of the following three core issues, and how they can influence our emotional state of being:

* Procrastination

* Time management

* Time wasters

And, with this added perspective on these three core issues, we will see how this helps to propel us on our personal path of enlightenment and self-discovery. How great would it be if as my wife often likes to say, "Time expands to meet my every desire." What if we could actually get a handle on and more control over the time we have in a 24-hour day? Priceless.

Procrastination terminator

Have you ever thought about what *procrastination* is really all about? It is putting off what you know should and could be acted upon now, until another time. This ultimately promotes feelings of guilt, disappointment, frustration, stress, and also confusion.

What actually causes us to do this? Things like apathy, fear, a lack of knowledge, a lack of importance, a lack of discipline, distractions, regret, embarrassment, or simply trying to take on too much all at once.

For me, procrastination is just another word for "fear." Many times I will be coaching a private client, and rather quickly from my vantage point, I can see where they have their strongest fears and resistance. How? Well, quite simply put, it's in the areas where they put off doing the things necessary to meet their goals and objectives.

It would be as simple as picking up a phone to make a connection, but if one of their fears is "afraid of looking dumb, or being embarrassed," then they will do all sorts of other things in order to avoid the pain and possibility of starting the conversation. I see this sort of thing all the time. But when we dig a little deeper to discover that nothing truly bad will happen by taking action, we get through those invisible barriers and move a little bit closer to the success that they are looking to have.

Time management

The way you *manage* time has influence over many aspects of your life. But, to effectively manage anything, you must first understand it. So, what really is time? The substance of time is simply, events in sequence. What are events? Everything that happens is an event. Therefore, life is made up of events in sequence—and there are two groups of events:

* Those we can control

* Those we cannot control

But, you can always control your attitude toward the events you can't control. Therefore, what is time really? Time is your life, and life is your time!

Then, what is management? Management is the art, act, or manner of controlling. What is procrastination? Procrastination is putting off what you know should and could be acted upon now, until another time. And then when you allow procrastination to be part of your life, it steals a valuable part of it.

Therefore, with the above understandings, what really is time management? Time management is the art, act, or manner of controlling the events in sequences that make up your life.

Conclusion: Time Management = Life Management or in other words, "Personal Success Management." So, let's take a moment to look at the biggest roadblocks we face in today's world when it comes to time—and more accurately known as procrastination points:

Top 10 Time Wasters
* Smart phones and mobile devices
* Shifting priorities
* Lack of priorities/objectives
* Attempting too much
* Television and other entertainment
* Ineffective delegation
* Cluttered environment/losing things
* Lack of self-discipline/procrastination
* Inability to say "no"
* Meetings

How often have you personally fallen prey to one or more of the above time wasters? I know I am often guilty of indulging in one or more of these. But, for the eventual success of our top priorities, it is essential to avoid, eliminate, and overcome most, if not all, of these distractions and time wasters.

Trust me when I say this is a very important element and contributing factor for those who succeed, and for those who fail. This isn't rocket science, but it is very important to get a handle on these distractions.

So, what to do? How do we build the self-discipline to stay the course and obtain the success we desire? In the following, we have outlined some very good ways in which to avoid and eliminate those activities that rob us of too much valuable time. Do what you can to follow these suggestions. It may seem hard at first, but as with anything of value or importance, there are things we must do and trade-offs we must face.

How to Overcome "Time Wasters:"

- Smart phones and mobile devices
    - o determine when is the appropriate time to use your phone and when its not
    - o learn good phone etiquette
    - o learn to be present in each moment and in each situation
    - o learn to let your phone wait when involved with other priorities—in other words, learn when to ignore it

- Shifting priorities
    - o make a list of important tasks to accomplish each day
    - o rank them in order of priority
    - o estimate the time required to finish each task—remember to be realistic and include an extra buffer period
    - o carry forward any items not completed
    - o use a daily planner

- Lack of priorities/objectives
    - o apply the principle of DEPUTIS to help clarify your vision of what needs to be accomplished
    - o set long-term goals, short-term goals, and then immediate goals
    - o set clear, realistic dates for accomplishing your goals

- Attempting too much
    - o time-frame your activities so you don't spend too much time on one task and neglect another

95

- learn to say "no"
- apply the 5 D's Principles: Decide, Do, Delegate, Defer, or Dump
- log it into your daily planner
- give yourself a break and some rewards along the way as an encouragement

- **Television and other entertainment**
  - determine how much time you can allocate to entertainment
  - engage in television and other entertainment only when it doesn't conflict with other priorities

- **Ineffective delegation**
  - the concept of leverage is an important one—work out how much your time is worth per hour, and if possible, delegate tasks that don't give you the highest leverage of your time
  - make a list of tasks you should do, those you can delegate—and to whom—and stick to it

- **Cluttered environment/losing things**
  - set up a filing system (or have someone set it up for you)
  - put a check mark up on the top of each document you handle—if you come across it more than three times and it can wait, strictly apply the 5 D's Principle

- **Lack of self-discipline/procrastination**
  - have a chart or visual display of an important project placed where you can see it to maintain focus
  - get support from a loved one or close friend to help you—if you are working on a project with other people, partner with one of them for mutual support; it makes the job easier to finish
  - be creative—make things fun to do so you want to do them

o if it's too big, break the task into smaller laser units—and reward yourself along the way

• Inability to say "no"

o ask for time to consider before you agree to doing anything—it's easier to say no after a realistic look at your schedule

o be honest—explain your situation and ask if you can work out an alternative.

• Meetings

o be clear about the reason for the meeting and the "desired outcome"

o time-frame meetings and make sure you start and end on time

o send out an agenda and related materials beforehand so each participant can prepare more effectively

So there you have it. My best attempt to provide you with the tools to overcome procrastination, eliminate time wasters, and develop some new time management skills. All of which will help you to achieve the goals you are setting for yourself, which in the end will make you very happy and productive.

EXERCISE: Make a list of your short-term and long-term goals.

Again, this is where you can get clear as to what direction you want to go in life, both professionally and personally. A short-term goal might be something like a specific amount of new income to buy a new flat screen TV or take a vacation to Hawaii. A long-term goal might be to launch a new business or to increase your current business by 50%. You can never have too many goals, both long-term and short-term. The more specific you can be is also important as it helps with the clarity of vision and getting into the feelings of having whatever it is you set as your goals.

Before we finish up with this chapter, I would like you to take out your "goal-setting" notebook again and get more clarity on what you would like to accomplish in this year and in the years to come. This is where I would like for you to get specific as to both short-term and long-term forecasting, and also project by project.

The way to achieve anything great is to have a target, then see that target as you are taking your shot at hitting the bull's-eye! Put those goals up there so you can see them—they are right out there and in your face each and every day.

Remember, sometimes you can adjust them along the way. But just like my son, Shane did in high school, even though your goals may seem pretty aggressive and perhaps unrealistic, by keeping them front and center you can able to find a way to achieve them even in the face of some real challenges and adversities. Give it a try and watch the magic unfold.

EXERCISE: List 5 reasonable goals to have for either this season or the next one—if you are an athlete, or if you are in business, list what your goals are for the quarter, or the next year, or even the next project:

This is where you can get really specific in certain areas of your life, whether that be in sports and/or business. Let's say you are in your first year in the minor leagues, and you want to continue to rise up in the ranks to reach the major leagues within a few years. You could set some specific goals such as 1) be a starter for the team you are assigned to, 2) make the all-star team, and 3) keep a positive and focused attitude throughout the entire season. Or perhaps you are an entrepreneur and you have a new product launch coming out this next year. You could set five very specific goals that will help ensure that your year-end goals will be reached and that your overall project launch will be profitable. Just make sure you are specific and provide details for greater clarity.

Keep in mind that your success and failure are in direct relationship to your daily habits. I once asked a group of athletes how many of them had a daily mental practice as part of their workout and training program. Out of the 300 that were in the room, surprisingly only three raised their hands.

Now, if that is the ratio standard, just be sure you are one of those three—that way I will at least know you have learned something from this book!

Again, there was something inside of you that inspired you to set these goals in the first place. So, who is to say they can't be achieved? Who was it who said, "If you can see it, you can achieve it!" Well, they were right on the money—especially when it comes down to achieving great success with incredible endeavors.

Why did you do that, dad?

There was a time when my father was asked why he put his life on the line. "Because I love God, I love my Marines, and that is where I was needed most." That is the answer he gave when my brother asked him, "Dad why did you lead the charge at Iwo Jima?"

And, that is exactly what he did at two very bloody battles—Iwo Jima and Saipan—when he didn't have to. You see, our father was a Navy chaplain and he wasn't supposed to go to shore in the first wave. Heck, he didn't even have a gun.

As the story goes:

It was late afternoon and wave after wave of hitting the beaches in one of the bloodiest battles in World War II had been going on since the wee hours of the morning. Finally the beaches had been cleared so the admirals and high-ranking officers could go to shore. An admiral yelled out "Where is Chaplain Austin? It is time to go ashore."

A young sailor approached the admiral and said, "Sir, Chaplain Austin went out on the first boat today." You see, Hammering 'Hank' Austin, as his Marines loved to call him, chose to lead the charge without a gun. By diving into the foxholes, he gave encouragement and communion to his men who were battling for their very lives—all in the pursuit of keeping our country free.

Take a moment to feel that same courage and bring it to whatever you are working on—and add in an extra dose of passion and purpose. "Where are you needed most?" What is it you would truly love? And, are you willing to take on machine gun fire to achieve it? Thankfully, and because of our soldiers and veterans, you may not ever have to take on machine gun fire.

You will, however, have to take on your own "fears" and step out of your comfort zone to achieve those goals you have set out to achieve. Each time you are tempted to give up on your dream, ask yourself this; "How important is it to me?"

If your answer is "This is where I'm needed most, and this is what I truly love," then step forward boldly in pursuit of your dreams—and, even in the face of fear, step forward with persistent commitment.

This reminds me of what the premiere scientist, Wernher von Braun, said to President John F. Kennedy when asked what it would take to send a man, and by the end of that decade, into space and to the moon, then return him safely back to Earth? Wernher von Braun said quite simply, "The will to do it." And, that is all it really takes on your part—*the will to do it* and the discipline to see it through to completion.

Purposeful Activity: With Clarity Of Purpose

Again, DEPUTIS is a system that clarifies vision and direction, and is also a tool for project management and delegation. You can use this system for effective achievement towards any goal—and whereby we first give a clear description of the goal, then record it's purpose. We see into the future as though it has already been achieved and record the positive benefits.

Implementation Checklist +Results:

* DEscribe what you are to do.

* PUrpose is the reason for doing it.

* TImeline is when it is to be completed.

* Strategy is how it is to be accomplished.

What are the results from all of this? By knowing the purpose, this helps clarify and paint a clearer picture, as well as motivate and open the mind to creative and lateral thinking. And then, by creating a timeline, we record a beginning and completion time for the goal.

Knowing when it will need to be completed, motivates you into action through a sense of urgency. And, since the mind is such a goal-seeking mechanism, when we implement a strategy, we are able to lay out a clear action plan to achieve, and effectively use the principles of RESPA within the planning stages.

"It is only when I overcome fear with a knowledge of who I really am and pit myself against the barriers of false self, that I triumphantly break through into the realm of the true me."

Closing Principle

COUR™ (The Lion)

■ ■

In This Chapter

* Learning what it means to be the king of the jungle
* Seeing how courage and confidence work together
* Discovering how to tap into the heart of a lion

■ ■

"It's one thing to teach a principle and another to live it, but the greatest by far is to so thoroughly be it that your very presence does the teaching."

– Roger M. Anthony

To be honest, I think that's my very favorite quotes by Roger. It is one thing to know something, but to be it so thoroughly *"that your very presence does the teaching"* is the ultimate goal. I can't think of one thing that can be more important. Especially when it comes down to your own integrity.

You might remember the old saying, "Do as I say, and not what I do." Many parents have been accused of this sort of behavior by their own kids. Think of habits such as smoking or overeating, and of course drinking and driving. Right, I know that sometimes it's hard to live our ideals and our principles, but when *"our very presence does the teaching,"* that's when we are living in full integrity and at the highest level. That is what we should always strive to achieve.

In fact, Roger was the best example of this principle. Just by being near him, you couldn't help but rise up into your own true brilliance, because his presence brought such great inspiration. Roger truly was a lighthouse shining the way so others could find their own light. I strive to be that kind of lighthouse myself.

And now, both Tony Bodoh and I are carrying on this torch with our Beast Mode LIVE corporate trainings. The more I work with Tony, I'm finding many of these same characteristics within him. Tony is so thoroughly living these principles, that our clients instantly trust him and know he is a man of his word. He doesn't just teach these principles, he lives them too. Thank you Tony, you have courageously stepped into some pretty big shoes, and are filling them out nicely!

King Of The Jungle

With that said, courage produces confidence, and this is a big key to effective leadership. So, let's roar like a lion and simply be in that moment where "we know who we really are." We are then able to take on anything that confronts us, because it's all about having the courage to go forward and do the things that we know will achieve what we aim to achieve.

The lion represents being "King of the Jungle" and is a great example of one who knows who he is and knows the power that he has by just being who he is. A lion's very presence does the teaching. All creatures that are anywhere near the lion, know this too—and show him the respect he deserves.

It would serve us well to be king of our own jungle, so when we step on the field and need to perform at the top of our game—whether in life or in sport—our roar sends a shockwave of power out into the world. Never forget that power. Show respect to that power, and know that you have it within you.

Courage Produces Confidence

You Have The Power Of The Lion Within

"Courage is not the absence of fear—but rather the idea that something else is more important than fear."

– Ambrose Redmoon

The above quote dovetails right into what we've been talking about here with all of the BE A BEAST animal triggers so far. As with our animal friends, it's not removing or denying the emotions or instincts that we have been equipped with. But rather, it's equipping us to direct these emotions and instincts into something that is helping us be productive instead of destructive.

Fear is going to be there, but what will we do when we are faced with it? Do we retract into a "fight or flight" mode and run? Or do we *move towards* whatever is opposing us? If we choose the latter, we can have that fear channeled in an appropriate direction to elevate our actions and performance—and use it actually as a benefit. Whether its angst, nerves, or fear of success, there's an underlying fear that we fight with constantly—as ironic as that sounds.

But, when we are able to take all of our emotions and in a moments notice with our animal mind triggers be able to snap our performance into right action and to a place where we can use emotions to our advantage—so they are productive and not destructive—that is when we are truly living these principles.

Let your beast roar

Okay, so we've now gone through the three steps of the "12-Step BE A BEAST Process." And, we've anchored them all with some pretty amazing animals as our overseeing guides. You started off though with RESPA the crocodile and INROCK the eagle.

Now, we're going to sandwich the crocodile and the eagle as one slice, and the other slice will be COUR the lion. The reason for the lion is that throughout the world, lions are known for their courage. That's one of the great things they're known for. It wasn't until I saw one video in particular, that I realized just how powerful a lion really is—especially through the actual roar of this animal. And, in this video, there was a lion walking into a river and it was being threatened by not just one crocodile, not just two crocodiles, but actually there were three of them approaching him.

Naturally, these crocodiles, who can be fierce in their own right, were really going after the lion. I thought, "Well, this lion's going to turn and get out of there in retreat." You know, he's courageous but discretion is the better part of valor. So, I thought he was going to turn tail and run. But instead, he just walked into that water. I mean, he had intense focus and just began walking towards these three crocodiles.

But, the crocodiles weren't feeling very threatened by this. They were watching him come in. They started to come towards him and out of the water. The lion kept walking in and then he roared. And, this was not just your average everyday roar, but was a roar that sent curdles into every fiber of my being. And as this lion roared, all three of those crocodiles just began to back away. It was such an amazing thing to see—the power of his full roar.

Having the courage and the desire

The beauty of all of this is we *are* being courageous in these BE A BEAST training principles—absolutely. We are being bold, while intentionally inviting in this idea of "moving forward" with our initiatives. And that means out there in the competitive playing field, whether that be on the sports field, in a business environment, or anywhere else within our lives.

Within our day-to-day situations, we can courageously say, "I know where I am right now, but I would also like something greater." Strategically and tactically we move towards something that's better than what we've achieved so far—and some of those initiatives are big. That takes courage.

106

Just like when one of my private clients and partner, who lives in Israel, set an intention to meet the president of her country. Efrat Avnor did not have any connections to do that, but she had a burning desire to reach out and affect people in a positive way through the use of these BE A BEAST principles—and she summoned her courage to do so.

How can you create more courage in your own life?

When you use these animal guides we have presented here on a daily basis, you become more courageous. You will trust in yourself more so it is easier to walk boldly into your dreams. Half the battle in life is becoming aware of your thoughts and how they shape your life. It is easy to fall back into your old conditional habits without paying attention to your thoughts. By paying attention to them, you become awake to your thoughts that lead to your actions that create your results. Simply by applying RESPA or any one of these animal friends at the right time will be a major "game changer" for you.

Efrat had a desire and set the intention to make this bold move, and sure enough, while using the principle of COUR to guide her way, she has now in fact met the president—and, she continues along her journey of helping the people in her country shift their mindsets in a way that empowers them. And, helps them live better and more courageous lives themselves.

How can I expect to have success if I am not very talented?

We are really no different than those superstars you see out on the professional fields, or those billionaires you see featured in Forbes magazine. By applying the animal instinct "mental mindset" success principles to all of your intentions and goals, you can most definitely achieve great success—and that is precisely what I hope you will experience once you put these principles into practice.

Both Roger and I have seen amazing results living these principles. MVPs have been named, millions have been earned, and championships have been won, all by using these BE A BEAST principles. And this is not just a one-time thing that happens only once in a blue moon. These sorts of results happen time and time again, and from people just like you and me.

107

Again, "champions are champions *before* they are champions." Which simply means, it's about what you do today. You don't have to wait for that championship game to arrive before you say, "I'm a champion." Own it today. And, be a champion every day—so that everything you do is at that level of *being* a champion.

So, enjoy this journey in the discovery of your "bigger you," which is that person who taps into their true gifts and strengths. That is precisely what the BE A BEAST training is all about—taking the action steps and using your time wisely without worrying about what you haven't done, but focusing on who you are and what you will be doing. It's not wishing you will be that someday. No, it's today—taking the action steps today to further your goals.

Here is a helpful positive statement I have my personal clients use and like to have them repeat as often as possible: *"I am actively taking the steps that move me towards the intentions I have laid out for myself and have stated clearly what I will do."* Try this out for the next 21 days and see what great things happen.

The Heart Of A Lion

Animal Instinct Principle: COUR

> *"To play the game at the highest level, one must be able to execute without having to think about it."*

– *June Jones,* former NFL quarterback and head coach

The name of our lion is COUR. And, C-O-U-R stands for courage; so COUR the lion stands for his courage. This principle encourages us to roar like a lion and be in that moment where "we know who we are" and we're able to take on anything that confronts us no matter what. Because in that moment, sandwiching all of these steps, it's all about having the courage to go forward and do the things that we know will achieve what we're entitled to achieve.

In other words, get out of the way because we're coming through. And, you too can be king of your own jungle—so when you step on the field whether in life or in sports, your roar sends a shockwave and that roar is power. Remember to never forget that power.

It's like when you are in fact "talking the talk," and "walking the walk," the lion is a great representation of doing that. The lion who faced those crocodiles was "walking his talk." He didn't back down. He roared, but he kept walking. So let's walk the talk of all of these animal instinct steps and do what we have to do in order to achieve our goals.

Be a king of your own jungle...

You can do this, just by knowing who you are and what you're truly capable of. I have an amazing story to share that illustrates this perfectly. The really cool thing for me is it's about my own son, Shane, who plays quarterback for the Cleveland Gladiators in the AFL (Arena Football League), and what my family and I were able to watch unfold on live TV from the comfort of our own living room last year.

This was Shane's first year as the starting quarterback for the team, which was having a perfect winning season that was a dramatic turnaround from the previous year when they ended 4-14 and in last place for the league. This was nearly halfway through their season and they were one of only two teams that were still undefeated—the other one was the Arizona Rattlers, who were the previous year's Arena Bowl Champion and perennial favorite.

So, here they are, 8-0 for the season and losing to the Philadelphia Soul, who was controlling the game to the tune of a 31-14 lead at the game's midway point. However, Philadelphia was never able to pull away from the Gladiators, who would soon outscore the Soul in the second half—and most of that would come in the last 52 seconds of the game.

What can happen in less than a minute

It was during that final minute when the principles of LASPRO™ (which you will be introduced to in more detail in the next part of this series) and COUR became the "game changer" for Shane. You see, in his pre-game prep and visualization process, he had set two very clear intentions. These intentions were anchored with two animal instinct principles: LASPRO (for the laser focus of the falcon) and COUR (for the courage of the lion). What that meant for him was to have courage in that game.

109

Earlier that day, and before the game, Shane was on our regular "BEAST MODE ON Challenge" group coaching calls, where he clearly stated to everyone on the call, "These are my intentions..." He put it out there and on the line for others to hear. This gave his intentions added power, but also helped him have the courage to stay focused on them—since the group was now holding him accountable.

What he committed to was that, no matter what was going on in the game, he would have laser focus. He knew that a falcon hits its mark every time, even while traveling at speeds of over 250 mph. That was one of his intentions—to have that sort of laser focus. His other intention was to lead his team with great courage, just like COUR the lion—and, to have the patience to stay strong throughout the entire game.

You see, as a quarterback, sometimes you get tempted to throw too soon—but what he needed was COUR to stay present and have the courage to stay in the pocket, even while their defense was closing in.

There's still time on the clock

So, what do you think happened? Let me share a quick recap of how the final minute on the clock played out. Still down three touchdowns, one of Shane's receivers caught a 19-yard touchdown pass with 52 seconds left, and an extra point pulled the Gladiators to within 10 points, leaving the score 52-42.

The Gladiators recovered their first onside kick attempt of the season, and with 24 seconds left in regulation, another receiver caught a touchdown pass to cut the Philadelphia lead to 52-48. A low snap prevented the Gladiators from converting the extra point, taking away the ability to tie the game on the final drive with a field goal.

Needing a touchdown, the Gladiators recovered the onside kick *again* and drove to the 11-yard line of Philadelphia with just 0.8 seconds remained on the clock. With time for one play and 11 yards separating the Gladiators from the end zone and maintaining their perfect record, Shane rolled out of the pocket to his right and connected with a diving receiver for a game-winning touchdown, making the score 54-52.

That play marked the second of six times that season the Gladiators won a game on the final play of regulation. This was the impact these principles had on Shane's mindset, and as we watched it unfold—the only thing we could say pretty much was "Holy cow, how did that just happen?" You simply can't make this stuff up! As far as I know, this sort of comeback had never been done before.

And so, this is a perfect example of just how powerful these principles are, and how you can stay in the energy of COUR, for example, even at the highest level and under extreme pressure moments. I'll always love what Shane said to his team in the huddle with less than a second left to play in the game. He said, "Hey, there's still time on the clock. Let's make the most of it!" And that is precisely what they did.

Daily habits = success or failure

So, now you've journeyed with us and have learned about six of our animal "mindset" triggers. But, how do you implement them into your life? You do that by making sure it's a daily practice. I always say you need to create winning habits—and winning habits are not something you just do once in a while. You do them every day. Your successes or failures are a direct result of your daily habits. So, set intentions and make sure you have a real clear vision. Then use these animal instinct principles on a daily basis.

You've talked about a visualization process, what is that?

In the next book within this series, we will talk about the power of visualizations. That is actually Step Four of my "12-Step Process." You've heard about how effective these visualizations are—and we've shared some of the amazing stories already as to how well they work in setting one up for success. Basically, visualizations are a way of putting yourself into that place where you can see it first in your mind, and then you go live right into your own video.

You have a real advantage here. I never knew any of this when I played professional tennis—and I never won big tournaments. Later on, after I learned how to get my mind seeing it beforehand and getting there ahead of time, that allowed me the freedom to achieve what I set out to do.

That's what it's going to do for you. And, another thing is in terms of winning habits, they are going to help you have more confidence in yourself. So often we think about the one mistake we made and that just buries us, rather than thinking about all the good we've done. That ends now.

Is a "Game Ready" the same as your visualization process?

No, actually they are different, but one goes hand in hand with the other for greater impact. We will dive into that more in the second book in this series, but for now, here's a story that relates to this. I had a client who was a college baseball pitcher and played for LSU. They were going on the road to play the Florida Gators, and during our "game ready" process I wanted to make sure that he was ready to face the fans who undoubtedly would be doing their signature "arm-snapping" gator thing—which as you can image can be somewhat distracting. In our visualization process, I not only got him feeling focused and prepared, but also used the animal instinct principle of COUR the lion. This was so when those "Gator" fans began snapping their arms and chanting as he was on the pitching mound, he would be able to just stare them down—much like a lion would—and let them know he was the "king" of his own mound.

So, what do you think happened? Yep, he had a stellar performance while also earning the respect of his opponents—just as he had seen in his pre-game "game ready." He used his roar (his true strengths) and simply pitched into those strengths. He had no other distractions—for he knew he was the king of this jungle—and simply threw one pitch at a time with the heart of the lion deep within each pitch.

Feed the good – starve the bad

Moving ahead, I'd like to see you focus more on what you have and what you want to accomplish. When you start living in that positive energy, that's when you really start elevating because what you feed will grow, and what you starve will die. Let's feed the good that's in you now and expand on it. Let's grow it.

Use the principles that we've talked about, these tools that we've given you, and you'll find yourself playing at the highest level every day—not just once in awhile. Your consistency will increase, and you will rise up to where you're having the most fun in your life.

112

As you've heard me say and numerous times before, "Champions are Champions *before* they're Champions!" This simply means—it's what you do today that matters most. You don't have to wait to win a championship before knowing that "I'm a champion." Stand tall in that truth. Know it and own it today.

Be a champion now in everything you do—by having the courage of COUR the lion, and being the true champion that you already are.

Problem Solve: Through Opportunity-Focused Acts

Applying oneself through *courage* raises SAPA (Self-Awareness and Positive Attitude) levels, increases motivation, and eliminates procrastination so that we can act on any plan with laser-like focus on each strategic step, and effectively delegate and motivate. When you apply yourself through courage, this produces confidence. And always remember, that courage is a major key to effective leadership.

Implementation Checklist +Results:

* Do what you fear or dislike most (that which you know must be done) first!
* Look for the good in everything.
* Understand that with a positive attitude, all things work together for good.

What are the results of this? It reduces procrastination and makes the rest of each day a little bit easier. It also increases levels of SAPA and increases productivity. And, brings to you the awareness that all experiences assist to improve and prepare you to achieve more.

"I destroy the strongholds of fear
and doubt with the weapons of
commitment, action and persistence,
allowing success to occupy what
was once held by failure."

Afterword

The Rhythm Of Success™

▪▪

In Closing...

* Reviewing how to tap into your own potential

* Looking at how bold persistence can assist in your ability to thrive

* Seeing how cycles, rhythm, and systems can be designed for success

▪▪

"Ours is not to understand, but to do, and in the doing comes the understanding."

– Roger M. Anthony

Hopefully you have noticed by all that has been presented within this book, that the key to success is "getting your mind to work for you rather than against you." We have a gold chest in our minds—but, most don't know how to tap into these riches. The tools you have received in this "12-Step BE A BEAST Process," can completely shift your life for the better.

So with that in mind, let's keep it simple and pay attention to what we put into our minds. Is it positive or negative? Is it life giving, or life-sucking? Really pay attention to this. Be sure to keep a diligent watch over your thoughts—and to what you are allowing your mind to do *for you* in terms of creating a life you'd truly love living.

I always say, "Results are in direct relationship to your daily habits." This is true in both success and in failures. If you decide to put everything you've got into using these tools and focusing on creating new winning habits, you will shift your life towards having more and more success on a daily basis—guaranteed.

115

This is precisely why we created our "Beast Mode ON 30-Day Challenge." It keeps you focused and on track. And, it is a way to completely *bull-shift* your mind in a short period of time in order to achieve the results you are looking for—not only in sports performance and business endeavors, but also in your everyday life.

It has been my great pleasure to have worked closely with Roger Anthony in creating this powerful training. By combining Roger's 30+ years as a corporate trainer with my 30+ years as a mental performance coach for professional athletes, we found the magic formula.

The fact that we were fortunate enough to film the BE A BEAST training videos with Roger before his passing is a pure blessing I am so grateful to have received—and this is a blessing for you as well.

Tapping Into Our Potential

So again, we really can "get our minds to work for us" and these are the methods to help you do just that. As you learn more about them and use these tools, you will see there is a "Rhythm to Success." And the more you know this, the more you are able to tap into your true potential—and find your true gifts residing within.

The more you use these BE A BEAST principles, the more often you will have great things just show up "out of the blue." I just love it when that happens. Things just literally seem to appear "out of the blue" and your life simply gets better and better. Now, don't confuse this with the term "overnight success." True success comes from daily habits, mental preparation, and steadfast determination.

In reality, they aren't "overnight success" stories—they are all works in progress. First, they began as a seed of thought, then once planted in fertile soil, began to grow, and through continued mental focus, discipline, and real courage, they grew into the great stories that we all hear about and which only appear to have been "overnight" successes. Again, it takes daily practice, mental preparation, and steadfast determination.

Which reminds me of a great statement by Seneca the Younger, a Roman philosopher when he said, "Luck is what happens when preparation meets opportunity." Preparing for success is exactly what you are doing by using these BE A BEAST principles.

This is also why so many of our "30-Day Challenge" members stay on and go through the program time and time again. Why? Because they love staying in the energy of success. It's just like when I have a problem with my car and need to take it in for repairs. The mechanic is trained to take a look at a car and know what needs to be done in order to keep it running at optimal levels.

Many times, he can simply hear my car's engine and can pretty much know what is going on, what's wrong, and what needs to be fixed.

Why? Because he has studied it, and is in it every day. He knows the rhythm of a successful engine. Or, if I go to a heart doctor, he understands the rhythm of a heart and whether it's healthy—or not. Again, why is that? Because he has studied this, and is in it each and every day. He knows the rhythm of a successful and healthy life.

By simply listening with a trained ear, a mechanic can tell what is going on with your car's engine. A cardiologist can tell what's going on with your heart and your health.

Strongholds Of Success

Adapt & Thrive Through Bold Persistence
"I destroy the strongholds of fear and doubt with the weapons of commitment, action and persistence, allowing success to occupy what was once held by failure. Now I understand, failure must at all times give way to success through bold persistence."

– Roger M. Anthony

Over the years, both Roger and I have studied why some people become very successful and others don't. In fact, we've taken this combined knowledge and have used it to determine what exactly is the true rhythm of success—and believe me, there is in fact a rhythm to it.

117

And, just by talking with my personal clients and students, I can quickly tell where there is a rattle and where their rhythms are off. When I say we have a treasure chest right between our own ears, I really mean that. Our minds are filled with untapped gold just waiting to be discovered. And sometimes, it only needs a fine-tuning.

Just like with our NOBO principal where we talked about the miners search for riches but they stopped just three feet from the biggest vein during the great "gold rush," we want to get an expert to guide our way and help us to make those millimeter adjustments. That's how we tap into the riches and rhythm of success we seek. We get a coach to help us find our way. They know the rhythm, because they have studied it, and are in it each and every day.

We have the same abilities as that person who bought the original miners' claim for pennies on the dollar. We can seek out those who know more than we do and can help guide us to success. And you now are learning these animal instinct mind triggers that can help you stay in the rhythm of success along your own journey.

Modeling behaviors and animal instincts
That's why we call this training BE A BEAST. We have studied the animal kingdom and have found the perfect guides teach us there is more than meets the eye. You are finding the magic within these "beastly" animals for yourself. When we take the time and allow them to, they can guide us in every aspect of life—again, whether that be in sports, business, or in everyday life.

For instance, as you've learned, crocodiles understand their environment, adapt to change, and maintain a high degree of control over the circumstances they face every day. Don't those sound like tools we should adopt within our own lives? The ability to understand our environment, adapt to change, and maintain a high degree of control over circumstances are essential skills to have.

Now for the crocodiles, ultimately this meant they knew how to adapt and thrive—and it's the very reason they outlived the dinosaurs. And so, the first step in learning how to model their behaviors is to understand the rhythm of success. But, what exactly is the rhythm of success?

First, we must know that we are *designed* to succeed. Inherent in each of us is a motivating desire to achieve success. Intuitively, we sense that success is not only part of our mission on Earth, but it is our right!

And, an important element of our success design is our emotions. They produce an inner rhythm that acts as an indicator of sorts. They communicate our state of personal control, which basically means how well we are synchronized with our true identity. Our emotions ultimately help us measure our degree of success and fulfillment.

When we are in personal control, the inner rhythm is synchronized with our true identity, producing inner contentment. When we are out of control, the rhythm is out of synchronization with our true identity. The result is inner discord and discontentment.

So, what is the trick? How are we to succeed?

Well, before we plan the "when" and "how" to achieve our success, we must first know *what* it is, and *why* we want it. It is by understanding the "what" and the "why" that creates a powerful vision. And as we saw with the animal instinct principle of DEPUTIS, the strength of your vision, in turn, determines the value we place on our goals. Which then creates the desire and motivating power to succeed.

Designed To Succeed

Cycles, Rhythm, and Systems

"The standards in which we abide create the quality, harmony, and security of our lives."

– Roger M. Anthony

All processes that govern life are cyclic, systemic, and rhythmic. In other words, life is guided, governed and controlled through systems that, when in order:

* Work cohesively with individual team members

* Create cycles of control

* Produce rhythm, harmony, and integrity

These governing systems are present in all life forces, including animal, vegetable, and mineral. They are active, and they involve energy that flows through molecular and atomic action.

Their cyclic nature is what allows them to continually produce action, just like a well-oiled machine. And the functionality of the cycles can be measured by their rhythm. Remember the example from before and take a look at how:

* A mechanic can tell by listening to the rhythm of an engine if an adjustment needs to be made

* A doctor listening to the rhythm of a human heart beating can diagnose a problem and recommend lifestyle changes to remedy that

* A business consultant can tell by listening to the organization's rhythm through the way the staff communicates with each other can tell if their culture is cohesive and harmonious or not

What does all that mean? And how does it apply to your own life and circumstances? Much in the same way as those examples listed above, you can tell whether you are in harmony with your true self, simply by listening to the rhythm of your emotional system as it "warns" or "rewards" in the course of your daily life. And, it is important to note, that a healthy rhythm is both the prerequisite and the means for your success.

As said before, we are designed to succeed and to be in control, just like the wily old crocodile that's been around since the prehistoric age. Yet somehow, much of our lives are spent in the same kind of imbalanced, unrhythmic systems that eventually brought about the destruction of the entire dinosaur population.

When we find ourselves struggling against our natural design, we feel inner conflict because we're out of sync and out of control. Often, we pass this internal conflict into the external environment, rationalizing, justifying or passing the buck!

However, we are truly designed to succeed. How could we *think* otherwise?

Like all human beings, we are designed to succeed but, by allowing ourselves to be hoodwinked, we become conditioned to fail. Something has gone terribly wrong here! Even though we're designed to succeed, if we are not aware of "who we really are," we will never know what we are really capable of, where we're going, or how we are going to get there.

How a rhythm of success model should look

First, there are two elements that contribute to your governing beliefs and patterns—and which represent your governing values:

* R.O.C.K. —Receiver Of Correct Knowledge

* F.A.R. —Falseness Appearing Real, which in other words is being "hoodwinked"

From these established governing values, you will find either chaos or contentment. This is where you develop a "systems team." And, this needs to be a system based on integrity, or it will crash and burn.

You find yourself either in control or out of control. Your emotions then reward you, or they warn you. This is your body's way of monitoring where you are and it determines your level of SAPA (Self-Awareness and Positive Attitude). When you are "in control" of you emotions, it always increases your SAPA level.

Your emotional system warns when you are getting out of control and functioning against your design. And, it rewards you when you are in control and functioning according to your inherent design.

This system leads you to success (or failure), which if done well and on course, will lead to your ultimate desire in life, which is to find inner contentment. And as Roger so frequently said, to find "peace, happiness, and joy" or "PHJ" as was his favorite term.

In the end, if you are not fighting against yourself, you can spend time on what really matters. And, that includes being in the spirit of cooperation and collaboration with others. In other words, you can choose your reactions and actions to lead to freedom and growth—or you can fall into a pattern of restriction and lack of growth.

Where we go from here...

What comes as you discover more about "who you really are" and "what you are truly capable of" is a compelling and selfless desire to reach out in support of others by inspiring courage, confidence, and hope for their journey upon the pathway to self-mastery. In so doing, you utilize more of your real potential and move naturally towards the betterment of mankind.

As Roger says in his book called, *Now I Understand*:

To develop more wisdom, one must gather the firewood of knowledge, and ignite it by striking the flint of courage against the rock of self-discipline, thus creating fires of understanding. Wisdom, therefore, is knowledge on fire!

Now is the time when analytical logic must give way to the creative intuition. It is the time when the rigidity of the normal goal setting procedures and fixed plans will give way to the flexibility of intuitive visioning and inspired development, guided by the power of faith. These are the days of the new walk—the walk from within.

We encourage you to continue on your continued journey of transformation. You've now got new companionship with these animals as they help you navigate your own path. Your guides RESPA and INROCK, along with your other BE A BEAST friends, will be with you at all times. Allow them to inspire within you courage, confidence, and hope—no matter what. You'll be better able to help yourself, in order to help others along their own journey's of transformation—one person at a time.

Sneak Peek: BE A BEAST Book 2

DEVELOPING NEW WINNING HABITS...for your success. Discover that by using these "Winning Habits" as a means to get where we want to go, realizing attaining your goals and aspirations can become almost effortless.

Proven Results:
> *"Dave takes the mentality of the athlete to a higher level that I haven't seen before. He is definitely on the cutting edge of improving athletic performance through the mindset."*
>
> *-Chuck Long, head football coach and former Heisman finalist*

Step #4: Visualize Your Success in Advance.
Create the life you want by *seeing* in advance—your achievements, successes, and desired results, and then use this process to "live into your video." This is an extremely powerful tool that when used effectively and on a consistent basis, will dramatically enhance your life and get you the results you are looking for. In this chapter we discover that by using this process as a means to get where we want to go, realizing our goals and aspirations becomes almost effortless as they magically fall into place.

Animal Instinct Principle:
Valdepa™ (The Canadian Goose)
Value creates the *desire* that produces the *power* to *achieve*. The greater the perceived value, the more power behind your commitment and motivation to follow through towards your desired outcomes and vision.

Step #5: **Enjoy the Journey – But Also Enjoy the Battle.** Everything in life happens for a reason or has the benefit of providing an opportunity for learning and growth, so in this chapter we get in the practice and mindset of enjoying the process and enjoying the battle of our day-to-day experiences. Depending on your perspective, you can shift your attitudes and see the positive that can come from any situation or circumstance. Even though on the journey towards success, you undoubtedly will come upon detours that you need to navigate through, this process provides the method to maneuver around these obstacles and get you back on the main pathway to success.

Animal Instinct Principle:
OHWEL™ (The Koala)
Say "Oh Well!" instead of choosing to allow any
situation or circumstance to cause you stress and to
lose control. Choosing to remain in control of your
emotions when confronted with a challenge may not immediately overcome it, but it does place you in a position to overcome it! Always maintain control by remaining composed.

Step #6: **Being in the Moment.** How often are you waiting for something else to happen before you make your move? And how often do you find yourselves continually giving way to thoughts of what occurred in the past? This is the chapter where we dive deep into the process of "being" in the moment and being present wherever we find ourselves to be. When you worry about tomorrow, you lose a piece of today, and every time you get lost in the "what if's" of the future, you slip out of the present moment. So here we provide various methods for shifting you back into the present.

Animal Instinct Principle:
ETMO™ (The Hummingbird)
Embrace the moment! Each moment is a gift to
be cherished, not discarded by regrets from the
past or worries about the future. Jean de la Bruyere said, "Children have neither past nor future; they enjoy the present, which very few of us do." So respect and love life by embracing each moment.

To learn more of what our "BE A BEAST 30-Day Challenge" is all about, please visit: http://www.getbeabeast.com and for more info and other general updates, visit http://www.extremefocus.com

Acknowledgments

Foremost, we are so grateful to Roger's wife, Cindy Kang Anthony for her grace, strength, and inspiration. You are such a great support to us all, and from the depths of our hearts, we loves you forever and ever—and look forward to many more wonderful memories shared with one another. Special thanks also goes to our agent, Bill Gladstone, and to Gayle, for your continued support and belief in what we are doing—also many thanks to the entire team at Waterside Productions

Both Cathy and I will always and forever be grateful to have met Roger Anthony, for he had such a major impact on our lives—and still does. We met Roger in 2007 at a forum called CEO Space—thank you Berny Dohrmann for introducing us. We instantly became fascinated with each other's work, and even though we didn't know how or when, we knew we were meant to "unite and take flight."

Among other adventures, we had the great pleasure of traveling to China and India together along with our wives, and where Richard and Sally Crawford came along to film Roger and me on the "Great Wall of China," and where he also did his magic on the speed bag—while blindfolded no less. We also spent time together at the Forbidden City in Beijing and at the Taj Mahal in India together.

From there we went to Chennai, India and both of us were honored to speak at the World Women's Wellness Congress with more than 50 countries represented—that is where we also got to see the true brilliance of our friend and associate, Bob Proctor. Both of us had shared stages with Bob before, but at this event we really had time to have meaningful discussions over meals and excursions. Thank you Dr. P.I. Peter and Divine Noni for creating this special event, and for inviting us all to experience it with you. Thanks also to Bob who wrote the forward to this book, as I am always inspired by you.

"Success is the mastery of living in accordance with my created design and, in do doing, experiencing peace, happiness and joy, thus creating the harmony of inner contentment."

About The Authors

DAVE AUSTIN: (The Wolf)
Mental Performance Coach and Author.

coach :: athletes, ceo's and entrepreneurs.
athlete :: professional tennis.
trainer :: workshops, camps, and coach.
speaker :: international and domestic.
author :: songwriting for dummies (wiley),
the unfinished cross (hampton roads), the
law of business attraction (yinspire media).

Dave is a best-selling author and a "mental performance
coach" to elite amateur and professional athletes. As a
former world-ranked tennis player himself, he uses his
firsthand knowledge to help get his athletes "in the zone."
In addition to his one-on-one work with athletes and
businesses, Dave has among other things, helped the U.S.
Olympic field hockey team get their best results in World
Cup competition, and also assisted the L.A. Dodgers in
going from last place to winning the pennant.

ROGER ANTHONY: (The Crocodile)
Corporate Trainer and Coach.

mentor :: elite athletes and ceo's.
athlete :: professional speed bag champion.
trainer :: corporate, workshops, and coach.
speaker :: international and domestic.
author :: now i understand, tall poppies,
and rindin the puffer fish (CNWI)

Roger was the creator of the suite of Crocodiles mastery programs for corporations, adults, and children including Crocodiles not Waterlilies, Crocodiles not Dinosaurs, and the Crocpond brands, as well as founder of Crocodiles International, an organization that specializes in business and personal transformation. His innate ability to inspire individuals, groups and audiences worldwide ignited their creative intuitive nature in order to live their true mission and purpose in life. As an entrepreneurial coach of CEOs and founders, Roger's wisdom and wide contacts also enabled him to be an initiator of collaborative partnerships, often bringing together key team members and partners.

CATHY LYNN: (The Falcon)
Ghostwriter and Author.

author :: songwriting for dummies (wiley), unwavering strength: volume 2 (hasmark).
ghostwriter :: non-fiction, self-help.
screenwriter :: gracen returns home, without a gun, back from the dead.

International bestselling author of the book, *Songwriting for Dummies*, plus countless others, Cathy Lynn loves to create and inspire through her flair for writing; whether it's in her own books, co-writing projects for others, or through her passion for screenwriting. In her role as a ghostwriter, Cathy Lynn has co-authored several books with husband and mental performance coach, Dave Austin. Her clients range from Internet gurus, music-industry giants, and professional athletes, to relationship coaches and masters in personal development—her primary motivation being to help people get their stories told, which stems from her own dad's passing before he got the book he wanted to write out of his head and onto paper.

Dedicated to each other for more than thirty years, Cathy and Dave reside in Southern California, where they have enjoyed raising four amazing boys.

Extreme Focus

With over 60,000 thoughts a day running rampant within our minds, and it is all about narrowing down those thoughts and getting "in the zone." The zone is that magical place where everything seems to click, you are totally focused and nothing in the world can stop you from getting the job done. Extreme Focus not only helps you get "in the zone" but help you stay there longer while taking your game to the next level. The "Extreme Focus" approach to sports performance is based around Dave Austin's exclusive 12-step process. His methods are not considered ordinary, but rather the results he gets with his clients time and time again are quite extraordinary.

As Jim Tracy, the manager of the Colorado Rockies says, *"Dave works like no one I've ever seen before. But then again, he's the most effective of anyone I've ever seen in this field."*

Dave has had the privilege to work with teams such as the LA Dodgers and many top professional athletes in the NFL, UFL and Major League Baseball. So when the U.S. Olympic Men's Field Hockey Team needed a boost – they sought out his services.

Head coach Shiv Jagdav said of Dave's work, *"You could never pay enough for the value our team has received from this style of 'mental performance' coaching. This work is priceless..."*

Dave's mental performance coaching is in high demand, and up until now only a few elite athletes and sports teams have had the chance to experience firsthand his "mental advantage" – basically due to his personal time constraints of private one-on-one coaching. Now through the use of digital technology, Dave's unique processes and coaching methods are widely available to athletes of all ages, taking them all the way for Little League to the Major Leagues.

The Extreme Focus mental performance training products and online programs are designed to produce the same results Dave's one-on-one clients have enjoyed for years. Now it's your turn to get these same proven techniques and get performance driven results for yourself.

The Vision

Our students have the skills that make them powerful athletes and leaders; they know what they are capable of where they are going and how they are going to get there.

The Mission

We inspire and educate others through the latest technologies, utilizing proven mental performance principles that elevate performance, but also the ability to maintain better control in all areas of life and under all conditions. We train how to have your mind work for you rather than against you, and how to increase your level of focus to be more productive and efficient.

For more information on Extreme Focus and to read the "Weekly Current" blog postings or how to become a member for full access to all of our training videos, visit: www.extremefocus.com

The direct link to the BE A BEAST training videos is: http://www.videos.getbeabeast.com

For more info on our "30-Day Beast Mode ON Challenge" visit: http://www.getbeabeast.com

For more information on our corporate training programs visit: www.beastmodelive.com

Change Your Mindset: Change Your Life

It's time to bring out a whole jungle of wisdom—and BE A BEAST in everything you do.

Made in the USA
Middletown, DE
29 July 2016